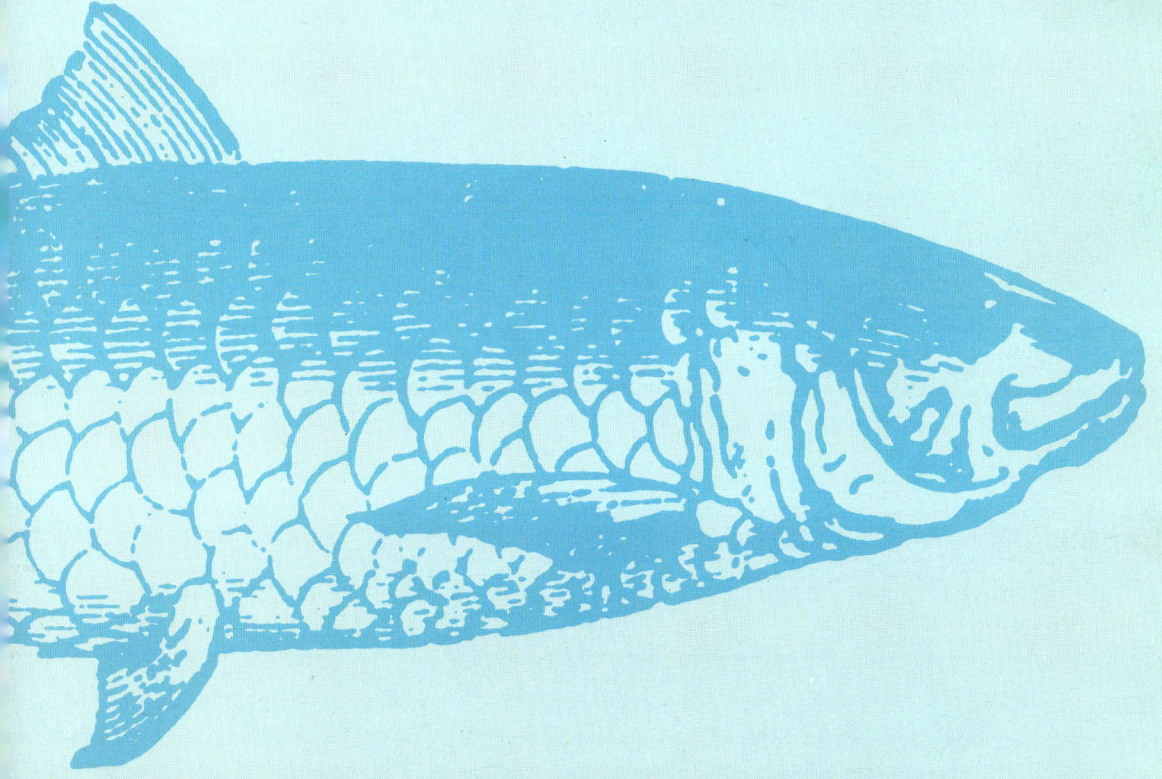

IDENTIFICATION
FRESHWATER

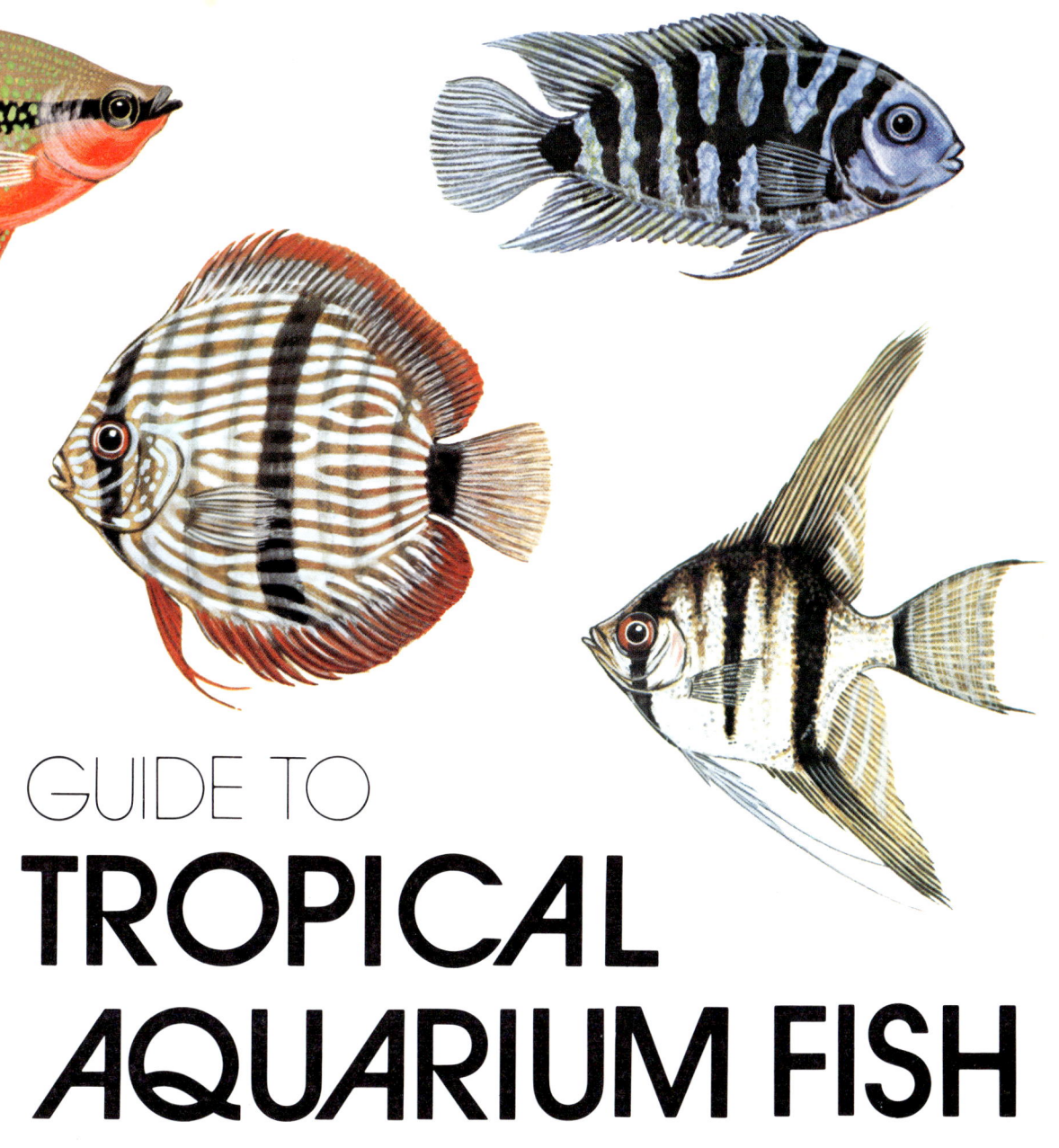

GUIDE TO TROPICAL AQUARIUM FISH

Illustrated in Color by Michael Stringer

ARCO PUBLISHING COMPANY INC
New York

© 1977 Blaketon Hall Limited

No part of this publication may be reproduced, photocopied, stored in a retrieval system, or otherwise reproduced without the express permission of the publishers in writing.

Produced by Blaketon Hall Limited,
for ARCO PUBLISHING COMPANY INC, New York

First Published in 1977 by
ARCO Publishing Company, Inc
219 Park Avenue South,
New York, N.Y. 10003

Library of Congress Cataloging in Publication Data

Pitcher, Frederick William.
   Identification guide to freshwater tropical fish.

   Includes index.
   1. Tropical fish—Identification.   2. Aquariums.
I. Title.
SF457.P55   639'.34   77–5519
ISBN 0–668–04300–8

Printed in Great Britain

Contents

8 Introduction
How to set up and maintain a Tropical Freshwater Aquarium

8 The Aquarium Tank

10 Setting up and siting the Aquarium

11 Furnishing the Aquarium

12 The Water

13 Water Analysis

14 Plants in the Aquarium

19 Filtration

20 Heating and Lighting

21 Buying Your Fish

22 Feeding

23 Breeding

26 Identification Guide

60 Index

Introduction: How to Set up and Maintain a Tropical Freshwater Aquarium

It is intended that this book should be used mainly by the aquarist as an identification guide to enable him to decide which of the many species of freshwater tropical fish available would be best suited to him. However, this brief introduction to the keeping of freshwater tropical fish will serve to whet the appetite of the aspiring tropical fish keeper and provides all the essential knowledge that is required. The task of reproducing and maintaining a simulated natural environment within the confines of a small aquarium should not be a problem for the aquarist who is prepared to set up his tank carefully and to make regular tests to ensure that a balance is being maintained. Once a balanced environment has been achieved, the successful breeding of fishes and the fascination of watching the fry develop is ample reward for the time and trouble taken.

The Aquarium Tank

Although freshwater aquarium tanks are not subjected to the corrosive action of sea water, they are still likely to corrode if water is allowed to come into contact with the frame. This corrosion is likely to release unwanted metallic salts into the water and cause pollution, and it is important that the frame should be completely sealed. A special aquarium sealant can be purchased for this purpose. It is sold in a special applicator that makes it easy to apply

THE AQUARIUM TANK

in a thin, steady stream. The sealant dries quickly but remains flexible, providing a strong watertight seal.

The aquarium tank is usually constructed from an angle-iron frame into which the glass panes are set and sealed. It is best to get the largest tank that you can afford. Good sizes are 30 x 12 x 15 ins and 36 x 12 x 15 ins, both of which are convenient and aesthetically pleasing.

In recent years the all-glass aquarium has become more popular, and aquarists are now beginning to realise that they are very much stronger than they appear and that they can be constructed in reasonably large sizes if the glass is of sufficient weight and the panes are joined carefully. Because all-glass tanks lack the rigidity which is provided by a frame, care should be taken to provide a firm and flat support for the whole area of the base glass. A large sheet of polystyrene laid beneath the bottom glass will effectively absorb any slight unevenness in the support.

To support the tank a sturdy base is required and these can be purchased ready-made, or they can be simply constructed. A very solid base can be formed from planks laid across building blocks. In the right surroundings, these natural textured blocks can look attractive but, otherwise, they can be easily disguised with wood facings.

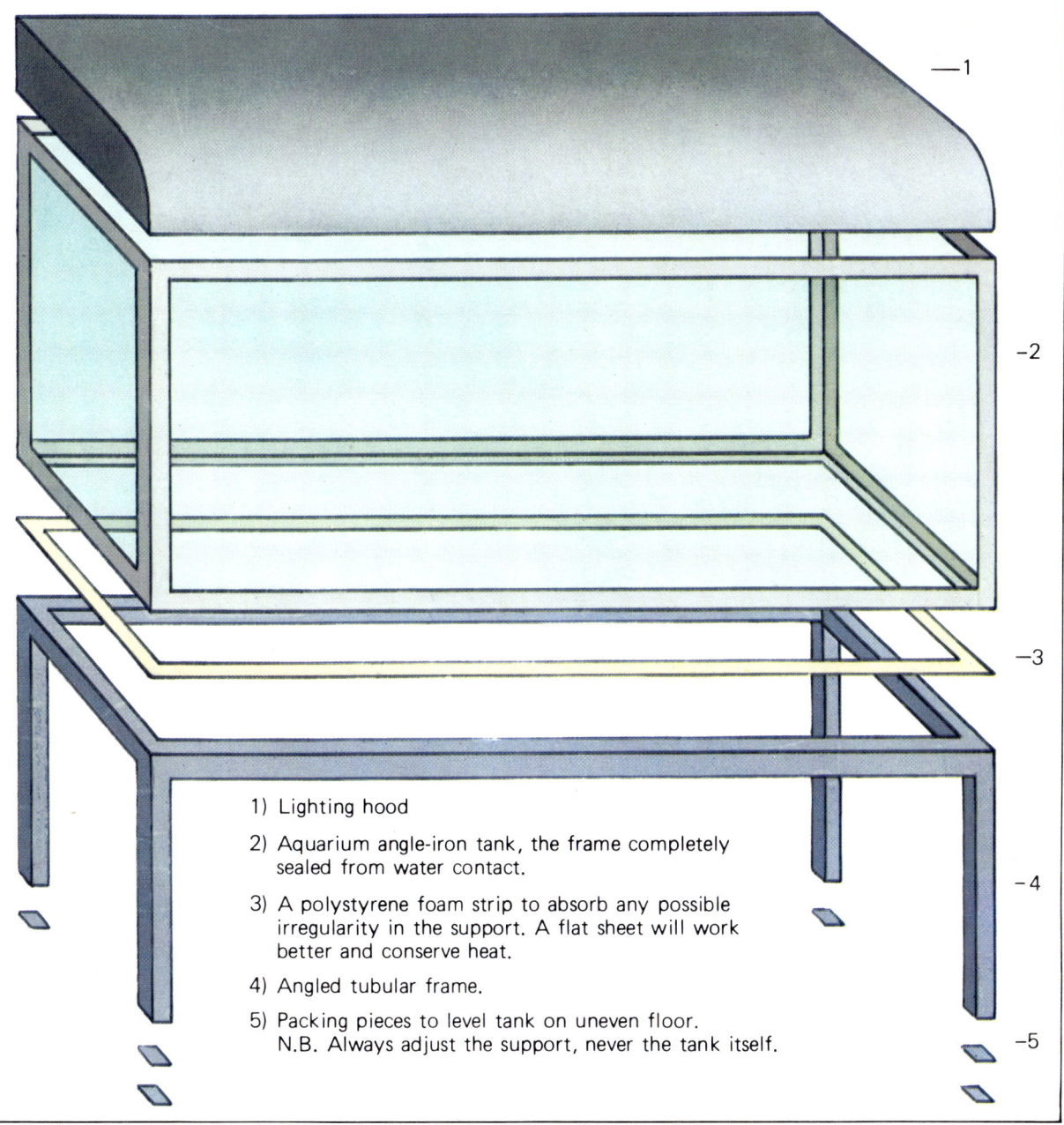

1) Lighting hood
2) Aquarium angle-iron tank, the frame completely sealed from water contact.
3) A polystyrene foam strip to absorb any possible irregularity in the support. A flat sheet will work better and conserve heat.
4) Angled tubular frame.
5) Packing pieces to level tank on uneven floor.
N.B. Always adjust the support, never the tank itself.

Setting up and Siting the Aquarium

When siting the tank, consideration should be given to the proximity of electrical outlets as they will be needed to supply power to the various electrical equipment required. A full tank of water is extremely heavy and cannot be moved without risking distortion of the frame and consequent damage to the glass. The tank should be sited away from direct sunlight unless adequate shading can be provided, since too much sun causes the uninhibited growth of algae and, in small tanks may cause overheating of the water. If you are a heavy smoker it is best to site your tank in a room which is not constantly in use, as your fish will not take kindly to stale smoke-laden air which can also cause a scum on the water surface. Newly-glazed tanks should be filled slowly to allow the glass to be bedded into the mastic by water pressure. Newly purchased glass usually has a film of greasy dirt over it and the panes should be thoroughly cleaned before the aquarium is filled. However, do not use proprietary glass cleaners which may leave some residue that could prove poisonous to the fish.

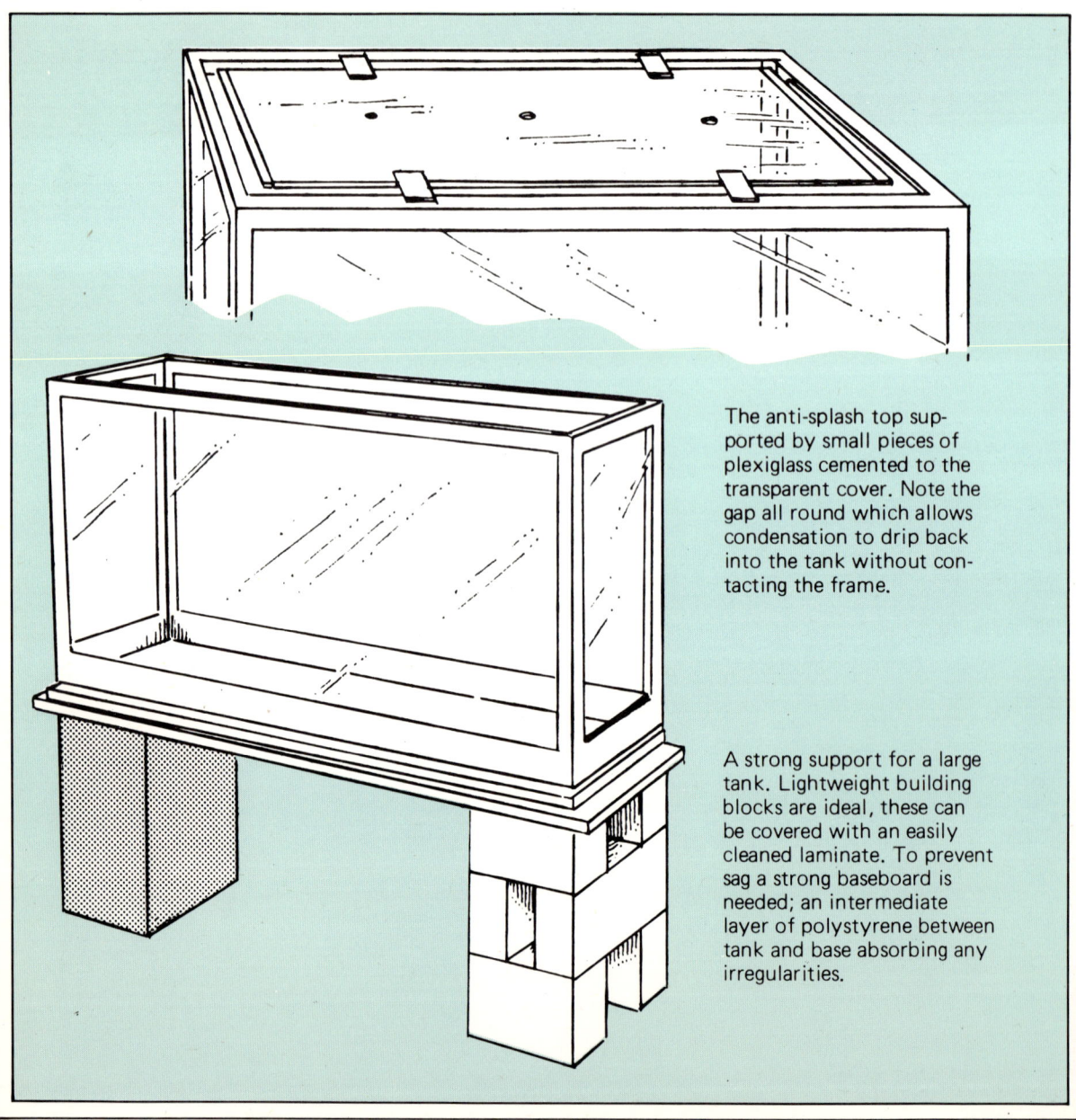

The anti-splash top supported by small pieces of plexiglass cemented to the transparent cover. Note the gap all round which allows condensation to drip back into the tank without contacting the frame.

A strong support for a large tank. Lightweight building blocks are ideal, these can be covered with an easily cleaned laminate. To prevent sag a strong baseboard is needed; an intermediate layer of polystyrene between tank and base absorbing any irregularities.

After the tank has been set up on its stand, some consideration must be given to the cover. The aquarium cover is necessary to keep dust and dirt out and also to provide a shade for the lighting. Between the cover and the tank it is usual to put an intermediate cover of plastic material. This is to prevent condensation from forming on the underside of the cover and on the electrical fittings. The see-through plastic cover should be cut 1 inch smaller all round the tank top and supported on small plastic lugs that can be glued into position. This gap allows condensation to drip back into the tank without contact with the frame. The outer cover containing the electrical equipment can easily be made from sheet aluminium. Alternatively, covers to fit standard size tanks are readily available from suppliers of aquatic equipment. It is advisable to have a small hole through the lighting cover, with a hole immediately below this in the condensation cover. This will enable you to feed the fish without removing the tank cover. Very large tanks can have specially constructed wooden covers. These should be made in several pieces which can be moved separately. When the tank has been sited, check that it is level with a spirit level. Any variation should be corrected by packing the supporting legs—not the tank itself.

Furnishing the Aquarium

If you have filled your tank in order to set the glass into the mastic the water should be emptied before the introduction of any furnishings into the tank.

Exactly how you furnish your tank is dependent on the natural habitat of the fish that you intend to keep. The composition of the material that covers the bottom of the tank is very important. Fish generally prefer a dark bottom covering and seem to thrive better in tanks that provide this. Conversely, in tanks that provide a light colored base the fish are restless and their coloration suffers. Since most aquatic plants are able to absorb nutrients from their leaves the floor covering medium is not so important to them as long as it provides firm anchorage for the roots. Exceptions are **Cryptocoryne** and most of the **Aponogeton** and **Echinodorus** species as these take their nourishment through their roots.

The undergravel filter should first be placed in position. The filter should be of sufficient size to cover at least two thirds of the base area. The filter is covered with gravel about the size of small peas, to an optimum depth of 2 to 3 ins. A layer of dark river sand can then be placed over the gravel. If smaller gravel is used, or if a thick covering of sand is placed directly over the filter, there is a danger that the interstices will become blocked; rendering the filter ineffective.

A variety of materials can be used to decorate the aquarium, but you should try to create as natural an environment as possible. Some rocks, e.g. granite, basalt, schist and red sandstone are especially suited to aquarium use. Others, including Ore-bearing rocks and limestones, are unsuitable as they are semi-soluble. Outcrops of suitably placed rocks can be used to conceal aquarium heaters and filter pipes. Rocks can also be scattered around the aquarium floor. In tropical rivers there is usually an abundance of tree trunks, twigs and branches that have fallen into the water and decayed. Therefore, pieces of wood in the aquarium help to recreate this natural environment. Because there is no flow of water in the tank, and because the volume of water is much smaller, the wood needs to be free from decay or pollution of the water can occur. Suitable woods are roots of beech, pine, oak and willow; preferably those that have already been in water for a considerable time. It is a good idea to boil the pieces of wood before introducing them into the aquarium, since this will kill any harmful bacteria or insects that may be concealed. The floor covering of the aquarium is usually sloped from the back towards the front as, besides providing a more interesting view, it allows debris to collect at the lowest point from where it can be easily removed. There is, however, no real reason why slopes cannot be made towards one corner or from the centre to each side. When choosing your plants consideration should be given to the fish that you will be keeping and the water conditions that you will be providing for them. Reference should be made to the section on plants before purchasing as some species will not grow well with others. The breeding habits of your fish will also affect the choice of suitable plants!

In nature, fish do not swim together except through choice. They are able to avoid community life if they prefer a solitary existence. Also, their natural habitat may have had many facets that were constantly changing. Sometimes dark and forbidding, sometimes bright and radiant. Again the fishes can choose between light and shade, and where possible these choices should be given to the inmates of your tank. Any book about fish is based partly on personal observations and partly on the recorded experience of others. In consequence, many errors of fact can be passed on. You should try to learn about your own fish and record their likes and dislikes. In a large tank it should be possible to give them a choice of environment; a shady, dimly lit corner with plenty of rocky caves, tangled branches or growths of plants where they can retire, safe from the unwanted attentions of other fish. The light can gradually increase to full brilliance at the other end, and it will soon become apparent which degree of illumination is preferred by the different fish in your tank. Watch, observe and, most important, record what you see.

After planting, the tank can be filled. When filling the tank, place a small bowl in the bottom and pour the water carefully into this, allowing the water to trickle gently over the sides. This will avoid disturbance of your bottom-covering material. When the bowl is submerged completely, then pouring can continue more quickly.

The Water

Although fish are able to survive in a variety of water conditions, success in breeding can only be ensured by providing the right water quality. Almost all tap water varies in quality and 'hardness'. Soft water is water that has very few salts dissolved in it but hard water contains a higher concentration of calcium and magnesium salts. The hardness of the water is caused by two conditions. Temporary hardness that can be removed by boiling and permanent hardness that is caused by sulphates, chlorides and nitrates that cannot be removed by boiling. Some tap waters contain substances that are artificially introduced and which render them unsuitable for use in aquaria. Although most fish are able to adapt easily to water conditions, if introduced to them gradually, it is recommended that those aquarists who are hoping to breed from their fish should take the trouble to set up their tanks with chemically clean water which can be adjusted to the balanced state required. It is far better to start with water which is unlikely to contain many harmful trace elements. Rain water, or water from mountain springs, would be ideal.

Some dark tropical waters, and indeed some moorland lakes, contain tannins. These are plant substances that can be extracted from wood, root and bark. A **very low** concentration of tannins has a bacteriostatic effect and can prevent the multiplication of certain bacteria. If fish that are accustomed to tannin impregnated water are kept (for example **Aphyosemion**) then a small concentration of tannins extracted from sphagnum moss peat can be introduced into the water. This material can be boiled in distilled water and the resulting extract added to the aquarium water. This should be done through the filter to ensure even distribution. Only sufficient to color the water to a very pale amber color should be added. If you are using a power filter, activated charcoal should not be used as a filter medium as this will remove the tannin from the water. In place of charcoal, sphagnum moss peat can be used and this helps to keep the water soft and slightly acid. Frequent tests of pH should be carried out to ensure that the correct level is not being exceeded.

The main factors affecting the suitability of water for fish keeping are: the hardness of the water—soft water being preferable; the pH factor of the water—pH7 or slightly lower is right. The pH factor is of considerable importance to the successful breeding of fish and the ability of the sperms to fertilize the ova is very much dependent upon the pH level being correct. Your fishes will probably be able to adapt to gradual changes in the water balance but success in breeding can only be assured if the correct balance is constantly maintained.

Green Water Occasionally, the water might become green. This greeness is caused by the multiplication of algae and although it is a nuisance as it limits visibility, it does not constitute a danger to the fish or plants. The remedy is simple. Switch off your lights for a few days and thereafter reduce the lighting until a clean water balance is maintained. Where plants require bright lighting, removal will have to be by filtration. Algae growth on the glass can be removed by scraping with a razor blade. Careful positioning of the lighting should avoid this problem.

All tanks lose water steadily through evaporation and this loss should be replaced regularly before it becomes too severe. Always top up with distilled water or rain water. The water obtained from melting ice that forms in your ice box is suitable but this should be warmed to 76 deg. F before pouring into the tank. Never top up with tap water as this encourages the build up of salts that cause water hardness.

Debris that falls to the bottom of the tank does no harm and gives the tank an established appearance. It should not be allowed to become too thick and it can easily be syphoned off, creating as little disturbance as possible.

Water Analysis

Initial success with your aquarium depends to a large extent on absolute cleanliness during the setting up process and the ability to maintain a balanced aquarium. At every stage during the setting up of your tank you should give careful thought to avoiding contamination by unwanted bacteria. Your hands should be washed carefully and thoroughly rinsed so that no traces of soap remain — particularly under the finger nails. Everything put into the aquarium should be boiled, including the sand, rocks and gravel. Only when you are certain they are clean should they be put into place. To create the useful bacteria necessary to the complete environment, your tank should be innoculated with 'live' sand from an established tank. This is the only material that should not be subjected to the boiling treatment. After a period of twenty four hours, or so, a bacterial bloom or cloudiness may appear in the water. This is quite normal and should clear after a short while.

After the filter and foam skimmer have been running for forty-eight hours the water should be tested to discover its acidity or alkalinity. This is known as its pH factor. The hardness or softness of the water is affected not only by the water itself, but also by what is put into it, including the gravels, sand, rocks and wood. Simple kits can be purchased which make the testing of water a simple task. The instructions supplied with these kits should be carefully followed. Most tropical fish are happy in a pH level of around 6.5 to 7.5. A pH factor of 7 is neutral. Less than 7 is acid and above 7 is alkaline. The adjustment to increase pH is made by adding calcium carbonate to the water — preferably through the filter, to ensure even distribution. Too high a pH factor is

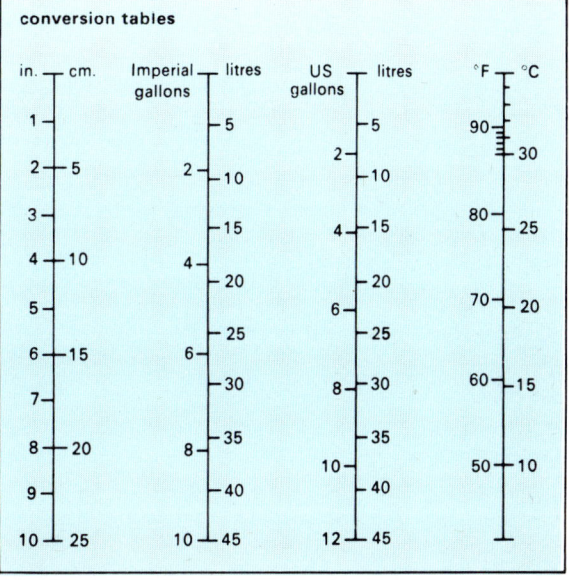

caused mainly by water loss through evaporation and the situation can usually be corrected by the addition of distilled water. Most tropical freshwater fish prefer water that is neutral or slightly acid. A very important factor in aquarium management is the limitation of nitrites to an acceptable level. The level of nitrites is indirectly caused by the activity of bacteria, but, after a variable period of time the water becomes stable or 'aged' and acceptable levels of nitrites are maintained. If fish are introduced into the tank before the balanced state is aquired losses are certain to occur. A kit to test the level of nitrites in the water can be purchased and the instructions supplied with it should be followed carefully and the results of daily testing recorded over a period of at least three weeks. From these records you will note that the nitrite high spots are at a level averaging 9 parts in a million and the low spots are around 3 to 4 parts in a million: sometimes less. When the water stabilises to this lower level your fish may be introduced. But never introduce stock before three weeks of continual operation of all systems. The introduction of fish into your aquarium is the culmination of weeks of effort and must not be rushed. Often the desire to stock the aquarium overides common sense and stock losses and disappointment result. Before stocking your aquarium make a final check to see that all is well. Examine your written notes, look at your pH and nitrite graphs. If all is well and they are steady the final step of stocking your tank can be taken. Remember that any last minute additions to rockwork etc. can alter the water balance and testing must begin all over again, so be sure to set up your planned environment at the beginning.

Plants in the aquarium

A well planted aquarium is not only attractive to look at, but easier to maintain. Plants take carbon dioxide from the water and convert it by a process of photosynthesis into oxygen, most of which is released into the water. This photosynthesis takes place only when the aquarium is illuminated. The amount of light required by plants varies from one species to another. Most aquatic plants are able to extract nutrients from the water through their leaves and do not rely on their roots for this function. There is also a wide range of plants that are able to extract nutrients with both roots and leaves and these are usually the easiest to grow in an aquarium. In order to thrive, some plants need calcium and others do not. Plants are therefore divided into two groups. Calciphilous plants, which are those needing calcium and, consequently, hard water and those that are calcifugous and require soft, slightly acid water. Obviously, plants from both groups will not do well in the same tank. Generally speaking, calcifugous plants should be chosen.

Before planting, any damaged or browning leaves should be cut off and the root tips trimmed to stimulate production of fresh root shoots. The correct planting is important and reference should be made to the diagram. Plants are very buoyant and may need stones placed around the stem to hold them down until the roots are firmly anchored. Plants should be grouped towards the rear of the tank, keeping the front free for swimming. It is better to buy two or three plants from each species, rather than single plants from a lot of different species. They are best planted in groups—all one species together, as this makes for a more natural looking arrangement. Give your plants room to grow according to their growth rate. Correctly planted and estab-

Calciphilous plants:	*Calcifugous plants:*
Vallisneria (fast growing)	Cabomba
Elodea	Cryptocoryne
Sagittaria (fast growing)	Echinodorus
Myriophyllum	Limnophilia
	Marsilea

PLANTS IN THE AQUARIUM

lished plants should grow well and produce new leaves regularly. If your plants are small and lack growth, it is likely that the water is too hard and requires the addition of distilled water, or rain water, to soften it. Algae growth on the leaves inhibits growth, but is difficult to remove successfully. Excessive algae growth can be caused by too much light and also by too much calcium in the water — both possibilities should be checked. The excessive use of peat extract can also inhibit plant growth and its use must be strictly controlled.

Some plants suited for aquaria

Acorus gramineus var. pusillus
Japanese Dwarf Rush.
Thin sword-shaped leaves radiate from this attractive plant. A variegated variety with yellow-striped green leaves is also most attractive. They prefer a well lit tank and water at around 59 deg. — 77 deg. F.

Aponogeton elongatus
Cultivation: Easy, flowers freely.
Grows to 11 inches.
Prefers well lit position.

Aponogeton fenestralis
Madagascar Lace Plant.
Cultivation: Easy.
Grows to 23 inches.
Does well in new aquaria and prefers a soft, slightly acid water.
Prefers shady position.
Temperature range 65 deg. — 72 deg. F.

Aponogeton undulatus
Grows to 9 inches.
Slow grower, ideal for small aquaria.

Cabomba aquatica
A beautiful plant but unsuitable for beginners. Difficult to maintain successfully.
Grows to 7 inches.
Prefers brightly lit position.

Ceratopteris Thalictroides
Indian fern.
Grows to 4 feet.
Prefers bright light, and water of 70 deg. F plus.
Thrives in soft, slightly acid water.

Cryptocoryne affinis
Water Trumpet.
Leaves about 6 inches long.
Grows well in subdued light and soft water.
Propagation is by runners.
Optimum temperature 77 deg. F.
A very attractive aquarium plant.

Cryptocoryne cordata
Attractive, undulating leaves grow to about 11 inches.
Subdued light.
Temperature 70 deg. F plus.

Echinodorus berteroi
Cellophane plant, Amazon Sword Plant.
Grows to 30 inches.
Temperature 68 deg. F.
Prefers soft water with tannin.
Well lit position.

Echinodorus paniculatus
Giant Amazon Sword.
Grows to 20 inches in good light and, therefore is more suited to a large aquarium.
Prefers soft water.
Temperature 68 deg. F.
Reproduction is by runners.
Easy to propagate.

Echinodorus tenellus
Grows to 3 inches.
A useful plant for small aquaria.
Soft water, peat filtration.
Prefers well lit position.
Will withstand lower temperatures around 59 deg. F.
Cultivation: Develops numerous runners.
Easy to propagate.

(Continued on page 18)

PLANTS IN THE AQUARIUM

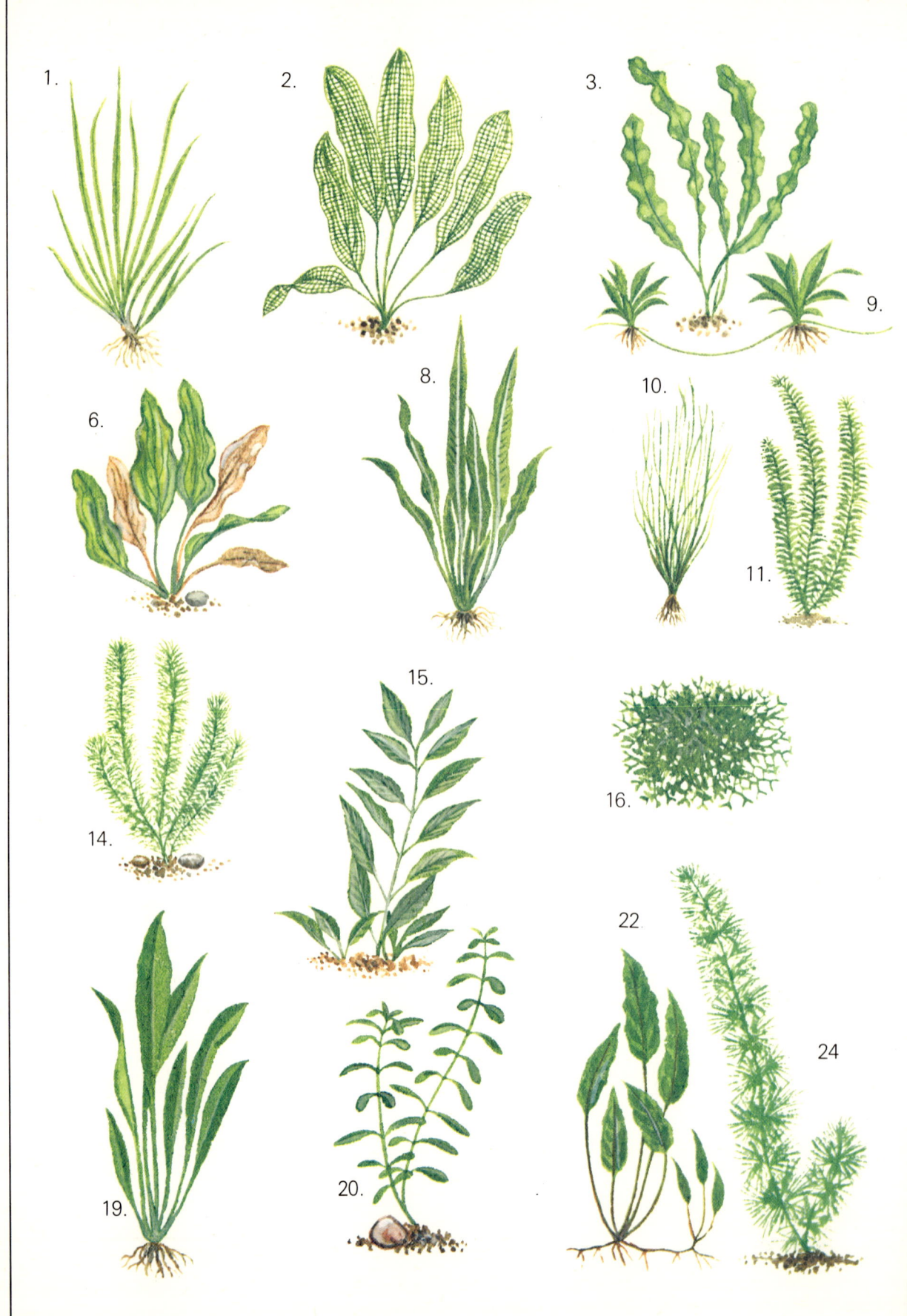

PLANTS IN THE AQUARIUM

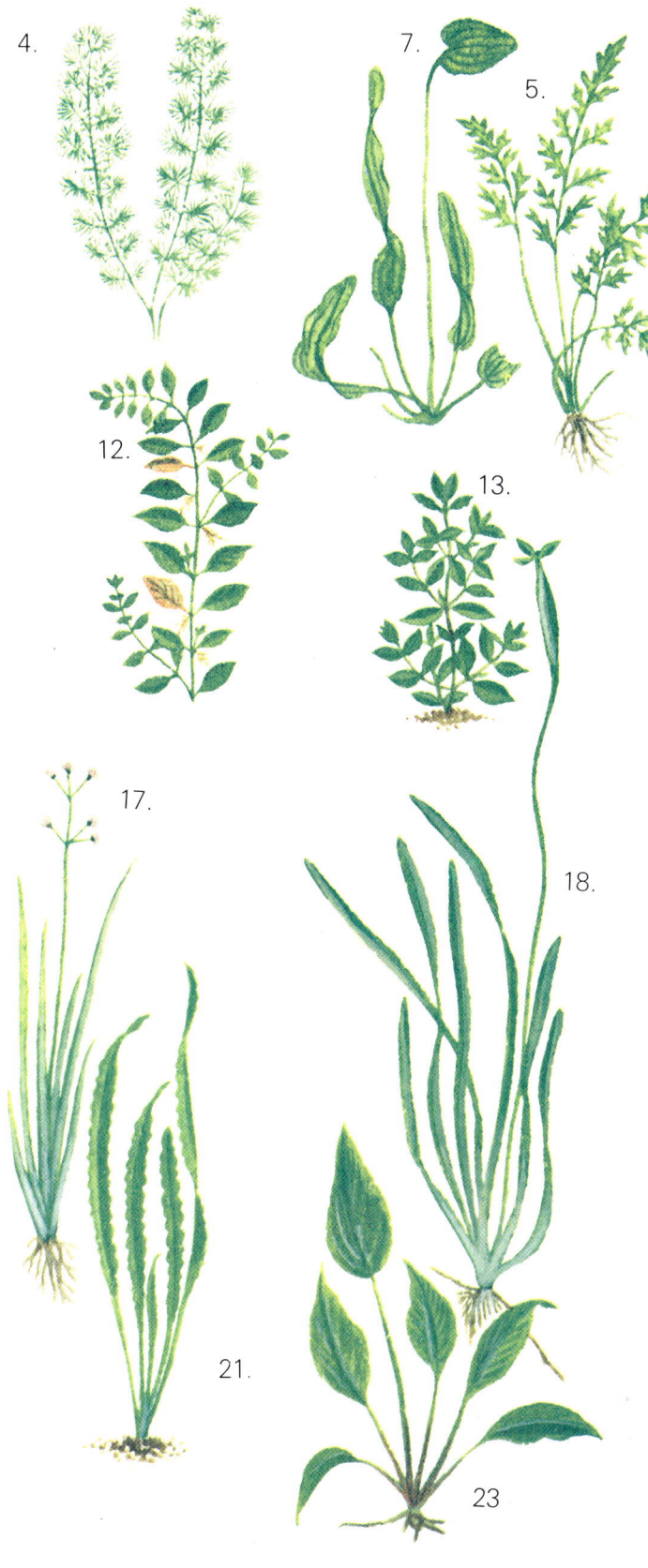

1 Acorus gramineus var Pusillus
2 Aponogeton fenestralis
3 Aponogeton undulatus
4 Cabomba aquatica
5 Ceratopteris thalictroides
6 Cryptocoryne affinis
7 Echinodorus berteroi
8 Echinodorus paniculatus
9 Echinodorus tenellus
10 Elecharis acicularis
11 Elodea densa
12 Ludwigia alternifolia
13 Ludwigia natans
14 Myriphillum brasiliense
15 Nomaphila stricta
16 Riccia fluitans
17 Sagittaria eatonii
18 Vallisneria spiralis
19 Echinodurus paniculatus
20 Hygrophilia polysperma
21 Aponogeton crispus
22 Cryptocoryne griffithii
23 Anubias lanceolata
24 Cabomba gigantea

17

PLANTS IN THE AQUARIUM

Elatine macropoda
Delicate plants which, due to their very small size, are ideally suited to smaller aquaria, although they are difficult to grow.
Prefer a brightly lit position.

Elodea densa
Argentinian Waterweed.
Easy to grow. Prefers brightly lit position with some sun.
Temperature anywhere between 50 deg. – 77 deg. F.
Good oxygenator.

Elecharis acicularis
Hairgrass.
This plant forms thick mats ideal for breeding tanks where egg scatterers are bred. Brightly lit position.
Propagation is by runners.
Grows to an average of 5 inches.

Elodea canadensis
Canadian waterweed.
Easy to grow but is more suited to cold water tanks as it becomes more spindly in tropical aquaria. However, it is widely available and often seen in aquaria as it is a good oxygenator.
Will tolerate a wide temperature range 58 deg. – 68 deg. F but will die in higher temperatures.

Fontinalis gracilis
Willowmoss.
Very small bright green leaves attach to long filamentous stems.
Does well in good light, providing cover for plant spawners.
Moderate temperature preferred.

Ludwigia alternifolia
An excellent aquarium plant. Easy to grow.
Brightly lit position.
Temperature 64 deg. – 77 deg. F.
Grows to 6 inches.

Ludwigia natans
Prefers soft water.
Well lit position.
Temperature 64 deg. – 77 deg. F.

Myriophillum brasiliense
Water Milfoil.
Grows to 4 feet.
A free growing plant that requires brightly lit position.
Propagation by cuttings.

Nomaphila stricta
Giant Indian Water Star.
Prefers soft water with peat filter.
Propagates by cuttings. Prefers well lit position.
Temperature 68 deg. – 86 deg. F.

Riccia fluitans
Cultivation: Easy.
Grows well in water 57 deg. – 77 deg. F.
Forms a thick mat which floats below the surface providing good cover for fry and for spawning.

Sagittaria eatonii
Grows to 6 inches.
Runners for dense mats. A slow grower.
Well lit, sunny position.
Do not plant with Vallisneria.

Sagittaria lancifolia
A robust, easily grown plant.
Only suited to very large aquaria.
Temperature range 59 deg. – 77 deg. F.

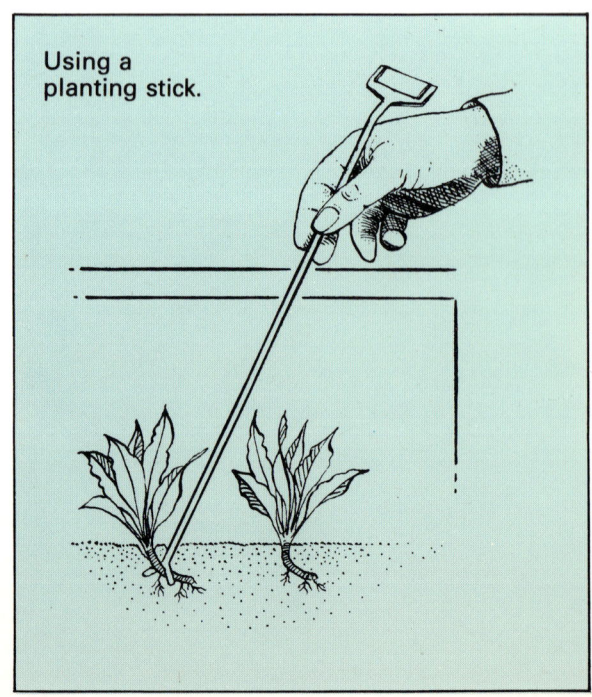

Using a planting stick.

Filtration

To ensure the removal of debris from the water and to assist the breakdown of harmful waste into harmless humus, an effective filtering system is required. There are basically two types of filter systems that have been proved effective and trouble free for the tropical fish keeper. These are the undergravel 'biological' filter and the power filter.

The subsand or undergravel filter has proved to be simple and reliable in small and medium sized tanks, particularly where the number of fish kept is small. It comprises a perforated plastic plate that sits on small projections which hold it about half an inch off the aquarium bottom. An air lift connected to this plate causes water to be drawn from beneath it and fresh water to be drawn through the plate and the covering gravel to replace it. This flow of water draws with it any suspended matter in the water, depositing it in the gravel where it is quickly broken down by bacterial action into harmless humus. The grain size and depth of material covering the filter is important. It should be about the size of small peas and have a depth of at least 2 ins with an optimum depth of 3 ins. A layer of dark river sand mixed with the gravel can be used in the top inch. One of the disadvantages of the undergravel filter is that it will need cleaning when it becomes choked. This may only need to be done after a year, or even two years, in a tank with few fish in it, but it will mean that the tank must be completely disarranged in order to clean the filter satisfactorily. The filter should cover two thirds of the tank base if it is to operate with maximum efficiency.

The power filter has the advantage that, being independent of the tank, it can be cleaned with little disturbance to the inmates. However, in a well balanced tank with an undergravel filter, the power filter is an unnecessary luxury. One of the more popular power filters is manufactured by Eheim and a range of sizes is available for tanks from 25 gallons up to 4000 gallons. When properly maintained these filters are noiseless and they utilize a sealed filter cannister which enables the pump to create a vacuum, causing the water to be drawn upwards through the filter materials,

An air breaker (left) and an under-gravel filter (below) with covering plate removed

A foam skimmer

which can be varied according to what is required of them. Before deciding on filter materials, seek the advice of your dealer. These filters can also be filled with high moorland peat which helps to soften the water and has a bacteriostatic effect. Be certain that the peat, if purchased from a horticultural source, does not contain manure or additives.

Aeration Although a certain amount of aeration is provided by the operation of the protein skimmer and the water returning from the filter, there is much to recommend the use of a completely separate air pump to provide streams of fine bubbles to help stir the water even further. It is certain that vigorous aeration is helpful to the well-being of fish and aids the dispersal of carbon dioxide which might prevent the saturation of the water with oxygen.

Foam Skimmer A foam, or protein skimmer is a water cleaner that collects contaminants from the water using a powerful stream of fine bubbles. It is an important device that is helpful in maintaining a balanced environment and its use is recommended.

Air pump A strong, powerful air pump is needed to operate both the foam skimmer and the undergravel filter. If both units are to be operated from one pump, a valve with outlets to divide the output between them will be required. It is better to use two separate pumps then if one should fail the other can take over until a replacement is obtained.

Heating and Lighting

It is extremely important to maintain a constant temperature in your tank. In tropical areas the water temperature varies only by narrow margins from day to day, possibly only 1 or 2 degrees. An aquarium heater will be needed to maintain a temperature of 76 deg. F – 78 deg. F. This temperature range is adequate for most aquarium fish species, although the requirements of some species are different. A large tank will probably require two or three separate heaters to provide even heating throughout and it is safer if each heater is provided with its own separately fused electrical supply. Then, if one should fail, the remaining heaters will provide sufficient heating until a replacement can be purchased. Two or three heaters are no more extravagant than using one as with thermostatic

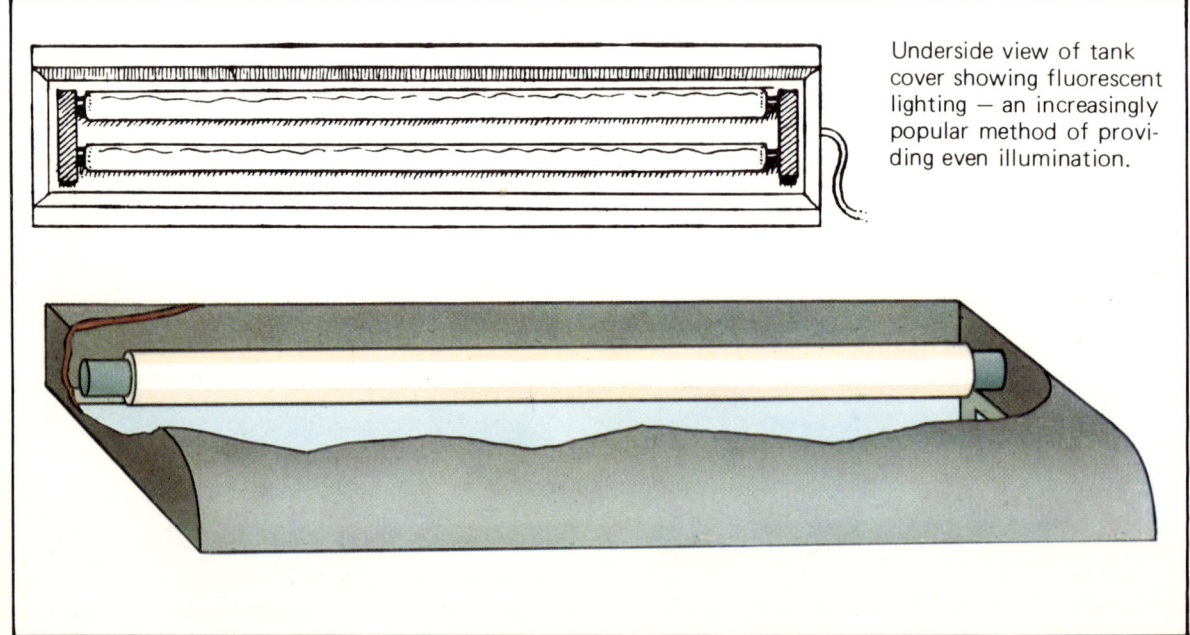

Underside view of tank cover showing fluorescent lighting — an increasingly popular method of providing even illumination.

controls they are in operation for far shorter periods at a time and are therefore less liable to failure. Heaters are available in different wattages to suit tanks of differing size. Although heaters are invariably available with thermostats incorporated in them, it is a wise precaution to have a separate thermometer from which the tank temperature can easily be seen. This should be positioned mid way between heaters. Heaters with reliable controls are essential if the temperature is to be maintained within close limits. Always take safety precautions before touching your electrical equipment. Turn off the power before making adjustments. If in doubt, consult a qualified electrician.

Lighting in your tank is essential if you are to show your fish to their best advantage. The hood covering the aquarium hides the lighting fixtures from view and serves to direct the light downwards. A wooden top can easily be made by the home handyman and the inside surface can be covered with baking foil to reflect the light. Remember that this foil may also conduct electricity so it is important that your lampholders are adequately insulated. To avoid algae forming on the front glass it is better to use a bright lighting tube at the rear of the tank and a dimmer one towards the front. This gives good overall lighting. It is better to use warm white or white tubes which provide a much more pleasant light than daylight tubes. The lampholders can be protected from condensation by a silicone spray available from your aquatic dealer. If the tank is placed in a position where it will benefit from 2 or 3 hours of diffused sunlight daily, this is a great help in promoting plant growth.

Buying your Fish

When purchasing a fish you should look for a specimen that shows erect fins, bright colors and which has a well fed look. Avoid fish that have sunken bellies or those that constantly rub themselves against rocks as this could be a sign of irritation caused by some disease. If any of the occupants of a tank look sick then it is likely that all the fish are carriers even though the disease may not be evident in all the fish in the tank. When purchasing for the first time, do not be persuaded to buy species about which you know nothing. It is better to go out with the intention of buying specific species that are known to be compatible. Try to buy

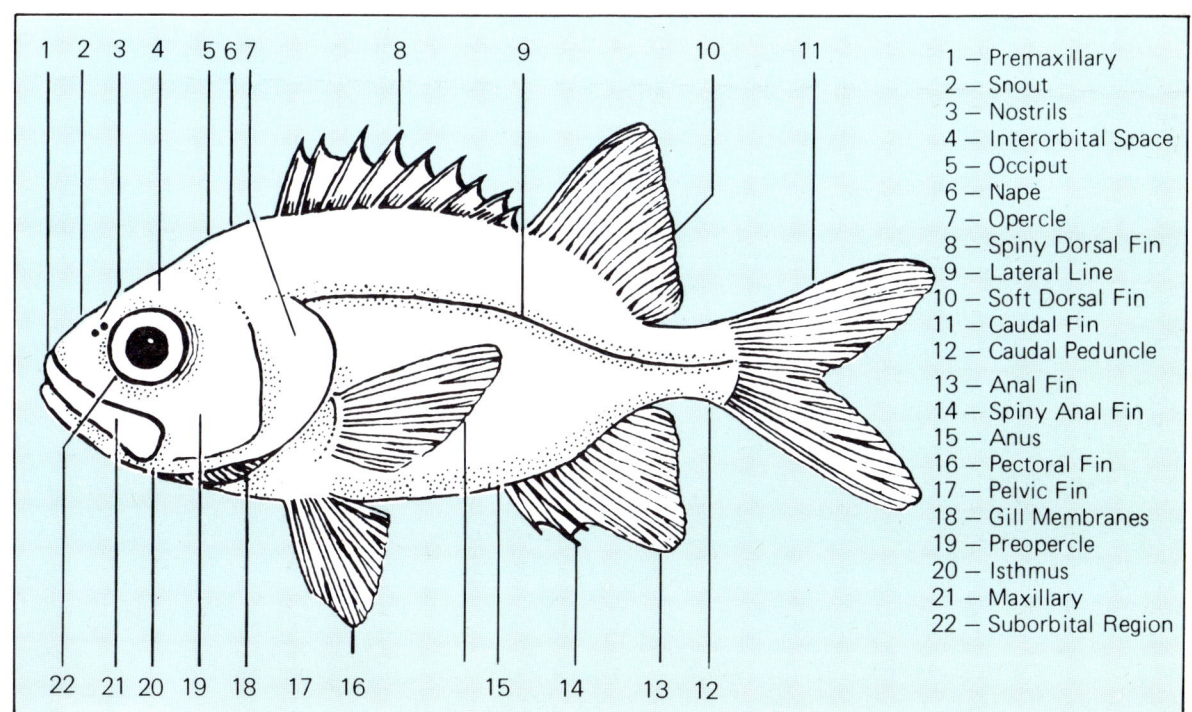

locally — the journey home will be shorter and the shock to the fish much reduced. Take a polystyrene lined box with you to retain the heat in the polythene water bag. Avoid unnecessary jarring and vibration and handle your fish like eggs. Choose specimens that are bright and active, clean looking and can be seen to be eating. Before leaving the store, get as much information as you can. Find out how long the fish have been at the store, where they came from and what they are eating. Also enquire as to the pH of the water in which they have been kept. Observe whether they are aggressive towards other fish and whether they have territorial inclinations. It is far better to make a preliminary sortie to the store on a fact-finding mission. Discuss with the store keeper the fish that you intend to purchase. Most are delighted to discuss all aspects of fishkeeping with a prospective customer. After all, you may become a regular purchaser at the store which gives you an informed and personal service. Beware, however, of the dealer who is not prepared to discuss his fish with you. There are some dealers whose knowledge is not what it should be and whose only purpose is to make a sale before their badly kept fish die in their tanks. Fortunately, these dealers are in the minority and their policy is a short sighted one as a buyer 'once bitten is twice shy' and will not return to their store again. If you follow the principles of good purchasing and set out to buy only the species for which you have planned a home then you should not encounter any problem that cannot be solved by careful maintenance. When you return home with your purchases, they should be introduced to their new environment gradually. The room lights should be dimmed, the tank lights switched off. The polythene bag containing the fish should be floated in the water to allow the temperatures to even up. Remember to open the top of the bag or the fish may suffer from lack of oxygen. Allow the water in the bag to mix gradually with the tank water and avoid any sudden change which might occur if the pH factors vary. Newly introduced fish usually seek the shelter of plants and they should be left alone for some hours, after which they may be coaxed from their cover by offering tempting morsels of food. Any food lying uneaten should be syphoned from the tank to avoid pollution. Remember to drop the food over a clear spot in the tank so that it can easily be recovered if necessary. Keep watch on newly purchased fish and see if they are aggressive or worried by other fish. If they are not compatible one or another of the fish should be moved to another tank. A well balanced community of fish can be obtained by choosing a bottom-living species, a shoaling midwater species and a surface-living species. In this way, they each have their own territory and the tank has a well filled look. Where possible, you should buy pairs of fish.

Feeding

There is a wide variety of tropical fish food available so that it should be possible to provide an interesting and varied diet that will keep your fish in peak condition. When you put a pinch of dried food into the aquarium, you will notice that it spreads over the surface and gradually sinks when waterlogged. It is better to limit this spreading by utilizing one or two floating rings that contain the food in one place. It can then be controlled and will sink over the clear area designated, where any food that is not immediately consumed can be easily found and removed later if still uneaten. Some fish feed at the surface, some in midwater and others scavenge from the bottom. The number of rings used must be related to the number of fish kept in order that both aggressive and non aggressive feeder each get their share.

Dry Foods
These are a useful standby and a supplement to a basic live food diet. Remember that dry foods lose nutricious value in proportion to the length of storage. It is better to buy supplies for a month at a time and from a store that has a high stock turnover, to ensure freshness.

Frozen foods: Brine shrimp, beef heart, shrimp, squid, lobster, oysters, scallops, sliced fish, sliced beef.

Live foods: Earthworms, daphnia, fruit flies, cyclops, mosquito larvae, white worms, blood worms, algae.

In their natural habitat, live foods would probably form a large proportion of the diet so it is reasonable to suppose that the provision of live foods makes for a more acclimated fish, with the possibility of improved fertility and breeding performance. Some live food should form the diet of all tank-bred fishes.

Daphnia are very tiny water fleas that can often be found in ponds. A large, very fine net will probably get you a good supply that you can then multiply in an old container in the garden, straining them out as required.

Brine Shrimps (*Artemia salina*) are an excellent food for young fish. They can be purchased as eggs, which can be easily hatched in a jar of vigorously aerated salt water at a temperature of 71deg.–75deg.F. They hatch in about 24 hours.

Rotifers These many-celled small animals are used as food for fish fry. Being very small, they are readily consumed. Collection can be made with a fine net, from ponds.

Whiteworms can be bred in boxes filled with damp earth and decaying leaves. They are very small, segmented worms, which grow to about an inch long. Although they reproduce and multiply rapidly, the culture eventually dwindles. It is better, therefore, to set up a new box in addition to the first after about four weeks, and to dispose of the first box after about 7 weeks. In this way, a constant supply can be maintained. The first culture can be purchased from an aquatic dealer.

Tubifex worms These can often be found in farmyard waste. They are small blood red worms which can be collected by flushing farmyard waste through a fine sieve and picking out the worms as they are exposed. Because of the nature of their breeding grounds, these worms should be thoroughly washed and fed to your fish sparingly as, if given too frequently, pollution can occur.

Earthworms are an excellent food for the larger fish. Red Oscars and similar fish devour even large sized worms in great gulps. Clouding of the water sometimes occurs if they are fed too frequently and care should be taken to avoid pollution.

Microworms are tiny, microscopic worms used exclusively as food for fry. Cultures are sold by aquatic dealers and they are easy to breed. New cultures need to be started as with whiteworms. In fact, they can be bred in the sour food remnants from a whiteworm culture. Excess food can be frozen, but this results in some loss of nutricious value and the constant feeding of frozen foods should be avoided.

Breeding

The breeding of tropical fish is probably the most rewarding part of fish keeping and about which many volumes have been written. The breeding habits of fish are many and varied. They can be live-bearers, that is they give birth to live fry, or they can be egg-layers. The egg-laying fish can be separated into various groups; egg hiders, egg guarders, bubble nesters or egg scatterers. For the beginner, the live bearers are the easiest fish to breed. The number of fry can vary from ten to a hundred, depending on the size of the female. Some easy fish to breed are Guppies, Mollies and Platys. When considering the large numbers of fry produced, the novice aquarist has visions of his tank becoming densely populated in a very short time, but, alas, this is not so. Unfortunately, the fry make excellent food and are quickly consumed, often by their parents, unless protection is given. An apparatus designed to protect the fry can be purchased and this is known as a breeding trap. It usually consists of a small plastic container that is clipped to the inside of the tank and into which the female is placed. The base has a grille through which the fry can go but the female cannot. She is then prevented from eating them. Since the use of this device is unnatural, it cannot be recommended. It is far better to observe and remove the fry if the parents' cannibalism is suspected. Eggs may be reared in a separate tank or small jar, with the water circulated by an air pump as this helps to prevent fungus growth on the eggs. Egg layers have a similar problem, as their eggs can also make a pleasant meal for the marauding fish. Once again, a square framed net can be clipped to the side of the tank, into which the eggs can be placed, if they are collected in time. The fry can be reared in the net prison until they are big enough to take care of themselves. Even at this time, unless the tank is thickly planted, the total number of fry will be quickly decimated.

Water temperature is very important in breeding tanks and unless you have the correct breeding temperature, and can maintain it to within a couple of degrees, you are unlikely to achieve success in breeding, even though all the other factors are ideal. A proper fish room can be a definite advantage as it permits you to have several tanks which can be maintained at varying temperatures and the results of breeding in each tank can be observed and recorded. If the outside lighting is kept very dim and the walls painted black, it serves to limit the fishes view to within the aquarium and outside distractions are kept to a minimum. Breeders who have taken this trouble report improved results. In aquaria, spawning is not restricted to certain times of the year as in natural conditions. This is because we are able to maintain a fairly constant temperature and the seasons are indistinguishable, one from another. In some live bearers, the females may show some changes in coloration which gives an indication that spawning is about to take place. Certainly, they become much fatter due to the increase in the size of the ovaries. The males, when ready to spawn, show a more marked color change and this acts as a visual signal to the females. Males that are ready to spawn become more aggressive towards other males that show the same breeding coloration.

When spawning takes place, the majority of species release their eggs into the water where they are fertilized by sperms from the male. After this, they are at the mercy of other fish, including the parents, who frequently consume them. Some fish species do not neglect the eggs but the male, or female, may stand guard over them until they hatch. This protection of the eggs seems to be connected with the number of eggs laid. The incidence of egg guarding is high among those species that lay eggs that are few in number. In some special cases, for example with cichlids of the genus *Haplochromis,* the eggs are sucked into the female's mouth after laying and are then fertilized. The young brood is not released

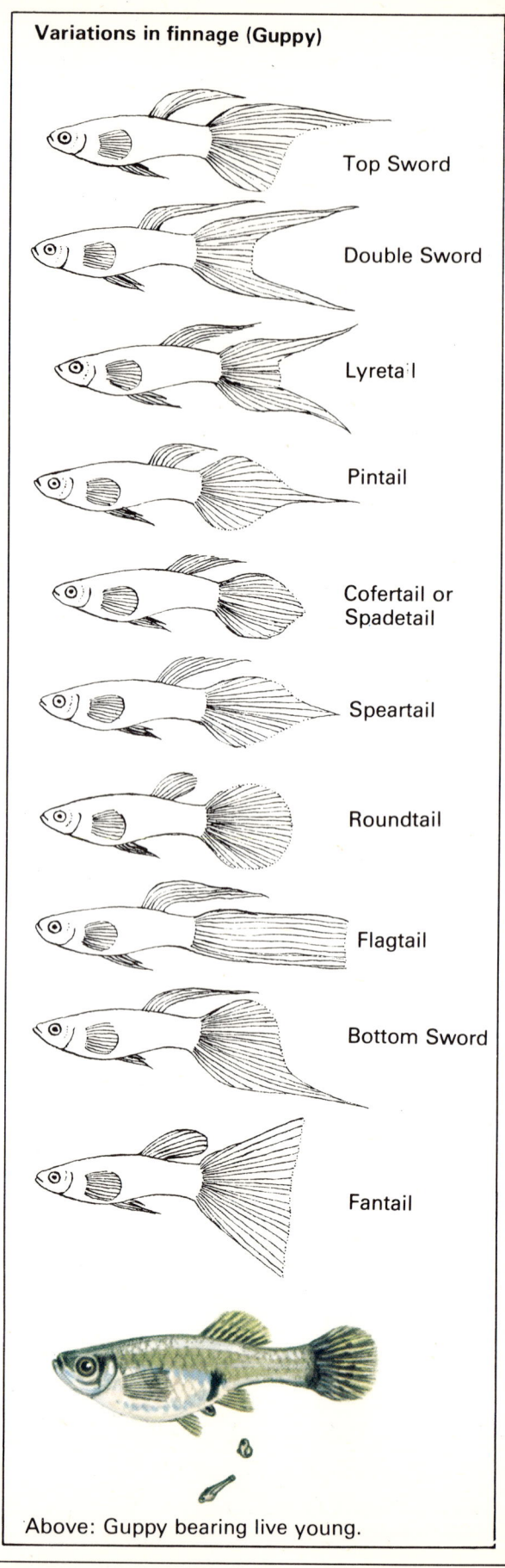

Above: Guppy bearing live young.

until they are able to swim and they then return to their mother's mouth for protection, if needed.

In live bearers, (viviparous), the eggs are fertilized within the body and develop in the ovarian cavity. The sperms which fertilize the eggs are released by the male through the gonopodium and travel up the oviduct of the female. The young are released as free swimming fry, which are soon able to find their own food.

The size of the breeding tank has a bearing on the number of fry a fish will successfully raise and on the number of eggs that the female will lay. A large tank will produce the best results. It is in the breeding tank that the importance of getting the correct pH and hardness is most essential. Some tropical fish hobbyists have a healthy, well stocked aquarium and yet they take very little trouble with getting the right water conditions. Their tanks are none the less beautiful and their fish seem to survive, but they seldom achieve the breeding results gained by aquarists who do take the trouble to provide exactly the right water conditions. The breeding of fish is a highly complex subject, every species having its own special requirements, that are beyond the scope of this book. After deciding on the type of fish you wish to breed, you should make a thorough study of the literature available.

Symphysoden discus
The King:
Discus or Pompadour Fish
Family: Cichlidae

Little wonder that this fish has been named the King, for it is both beautiful and interesting and comes in a wide variety of color forms. The colors vary according to its environment, food and habitat, making positive identification between varieties difficult.

Discus require soft water at a temperature around 78 deg. F. Feed Live brine shrimp, clean earthworms, white-worm and micro-worms. Daphnia are also readily accepted. The most interesting part of keeping Discus is their breeding habits. The eggs are laid on a vertical surface and hatch after four days; being tended and fanned by the parents. The free-swimming fry feed on food exuded through the scales of the parents, and can later be offered some brine shrimp, which, when seen to be accepted, can be fed continually until food of larger size can be consumed.

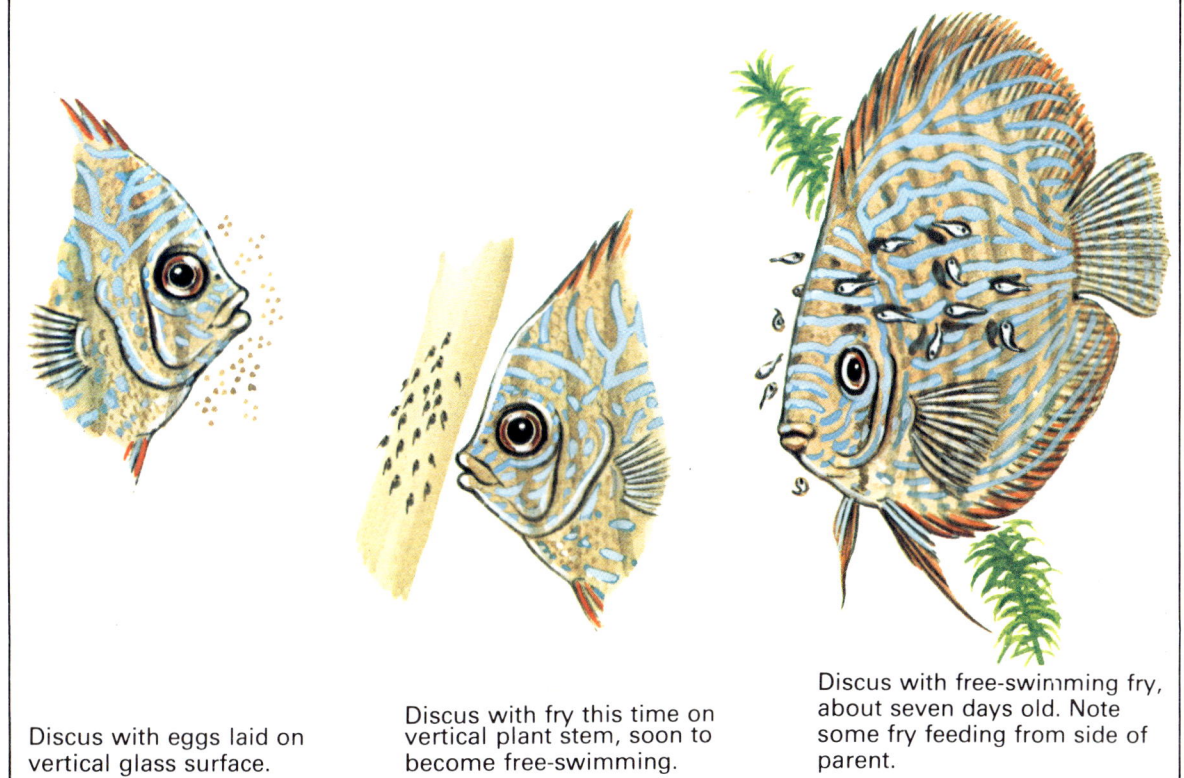

Discus with eggs laid on vertical glass surface.

Discus with fry this time on vertical plant stem, soon to become free-swimming.

Discus with free-swimming fry, about seven days old. Note some fry feeding from side of parent.

Identification Guide

Anostomus anostomus

Common name: Striped Anostomus
Origin: Guyana and Amazon Basin
Special feeding: Worms and other small food
Size: Grows to 7 ins and therefore suited to the larger aquaria. Peaceful when kept with similar fish

Aphyosemion australe

Common Name: Lyretail
Origin: West Africa
Reproduction: Oviparous. Egg scatterer
Breeding: Temperature 78 deg. F, Eggs hatch 12 — 14 days
Average temperature: 74 deg. F
Special feeding: Carnivorous
Community: Yes. Some fin nipping usual
Size: Grows to 2.5 ins

Aphyosemion bivittatum

Common Name: Red Lyretail
Origin: Tropical West Africa
Reproduction: Oviparous. Bottom spawner
Breeding: Temperature 72 deg. F. pH 7.5 Eggs hatch 12 — 14 days
Average temperature: 73 deg. F
Special feeding: Live foods, worms etc. Carnivorous
Community: Yes
Size: Grows to 2.5 ins

Aphyosemion coeruleum

Common Name: Blue gularis
Origin: West Africa
Reproduction: Oviparous
Breeding: Temperature 70 deg. F Eggs laid singly, hatch in 3 — 4 days
Average temperature: 72 deg. F. Dim lighting
Special feeding: Will eat small fish/fry. Carnivorous
Community: Yes, with similar sized fish
Size: Grows to 4.5 ins

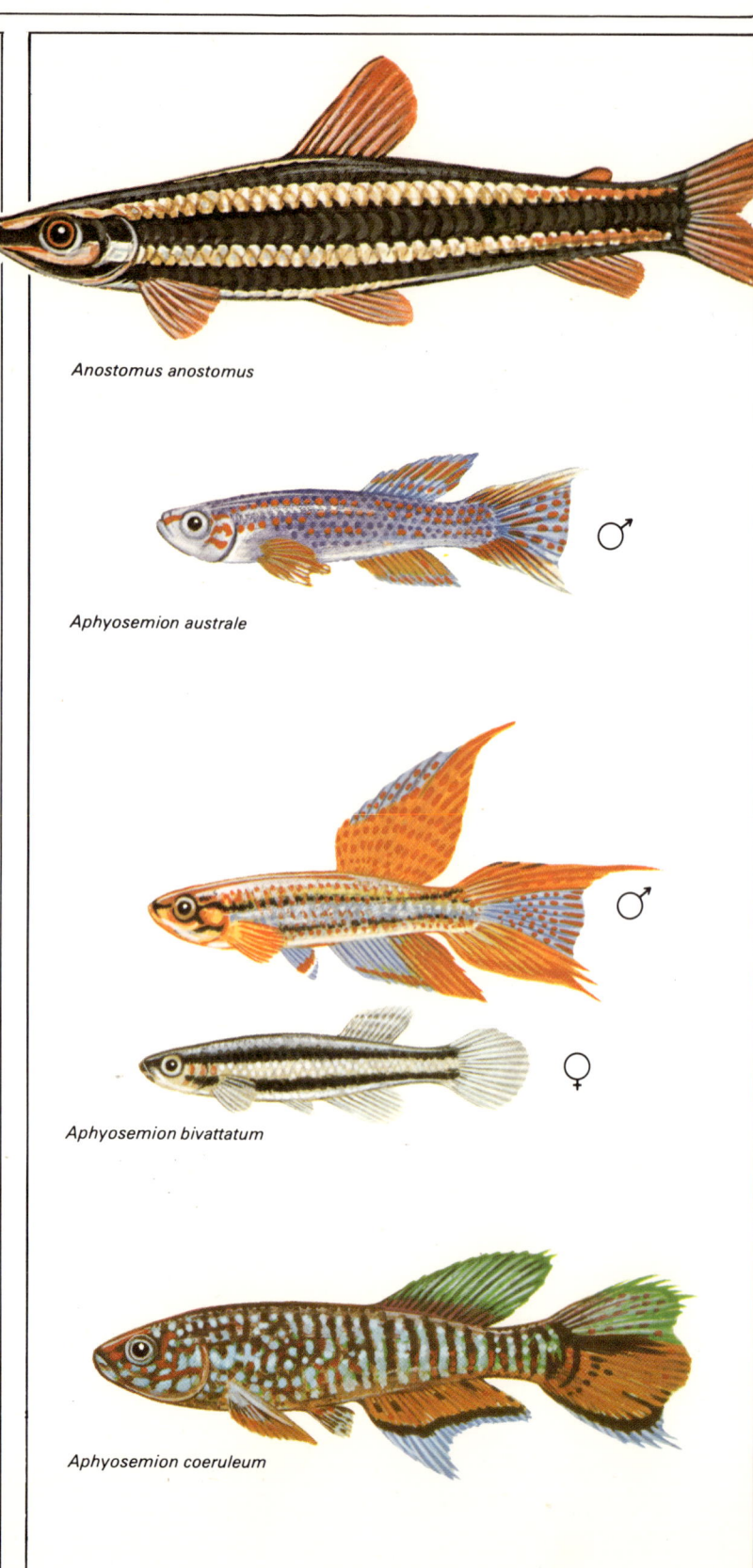

Anostomus anostomus

Aphyosemion australe

Aphyosemion bivattatum

Aphyosemion coeruleum

IDENTIFICATION GUIDE

Apistogramma ramireze

Common Name: Butterfly dwarf cichlid. Ram cichlid
Origin: Venezuela
Reproduction: Oviparous
Breeding: 83 deg. F Difficult
Average temperature 74 deg. F
Special feeding: Live foods
Community: Yes
Size: 2 ins

Apistogramma ramireze

Arnoldichthys spilopterus

Common Name: Striped Panchax, Red eyed characin
Origin: West Africa
Reproduction: Oviparous
Breeding: 78 deg. F Very difficult
Average temperature: 78 deg. F
Special feeding: Live food
Community: Yes
Size: 2.5 ins

Arnoldichthys spilopterus

Acanthopthalmus semicinctus

Common Name: Malayan Loach, Malayan Eel
Origin: Malaysian Archipelago
Reproduction: Oviparous
Breeding: Little known
Average temperature: 76 deg. F
Special feeding: Scavenger
Community: Yes
Size: 3 ins

Acanthopthalmus semicintus

Aequidens maronii

Common Name: Keyhole cichlid
Origin: Venezuela, Guyana
Reproduction: Oviparous
Breeding: 80 deg. F large aquarium preferred
Average temperature: 75 deg. F pH neutral
Special feeding: Live food essential
Community: Yes. Peaceful
Size: 4 ins
Choose strong rooting plants as cichlids are liable to uproot them otherwise.

Aequidens maronii

IDENTIFICATION GUIDE

Aplocheilus lineatus

Origin: Southern India and Sri Lanka
Size: Grows to 4 ins
Males are more colorful than females

Aplocheilus panchax

Common name: Blue Panchax
Origin: Burma, India, Malaysia
Breeding: Easy
Community: Yes
Size: Grows to 3½ ins
Color variable

Aphyocharax rubripinnis

Common Name: Bloodfin
Origin: Argentine
Reproduction: Oviparous
Breeding: 75 deg. – 80 deg. F. pH 7.5 – 8. Difficult
Average temperature: 70 deg. – 74 deg. F
Special feeding: Live foods
Community: Yes
Size: Grows to 2 ins
Breeding

When a successfully matched pair is found, spawning should take place in 6 ins of water at 80 deg. The fish jump clear of the water together, the female scattering the transparent eggs as she splashes back in. Eggs hatch in 30 – 36 hours.

Astyanax mexicanus

Common Name: Mexican astyanax
Origin: Mexico. S. United States
Reproduction: Oviparous
Breeding: Easier than most Characins. 75 deg. F
Average temperature: 74 deg. F
Community: Yes
Size: Grows to 3 ins

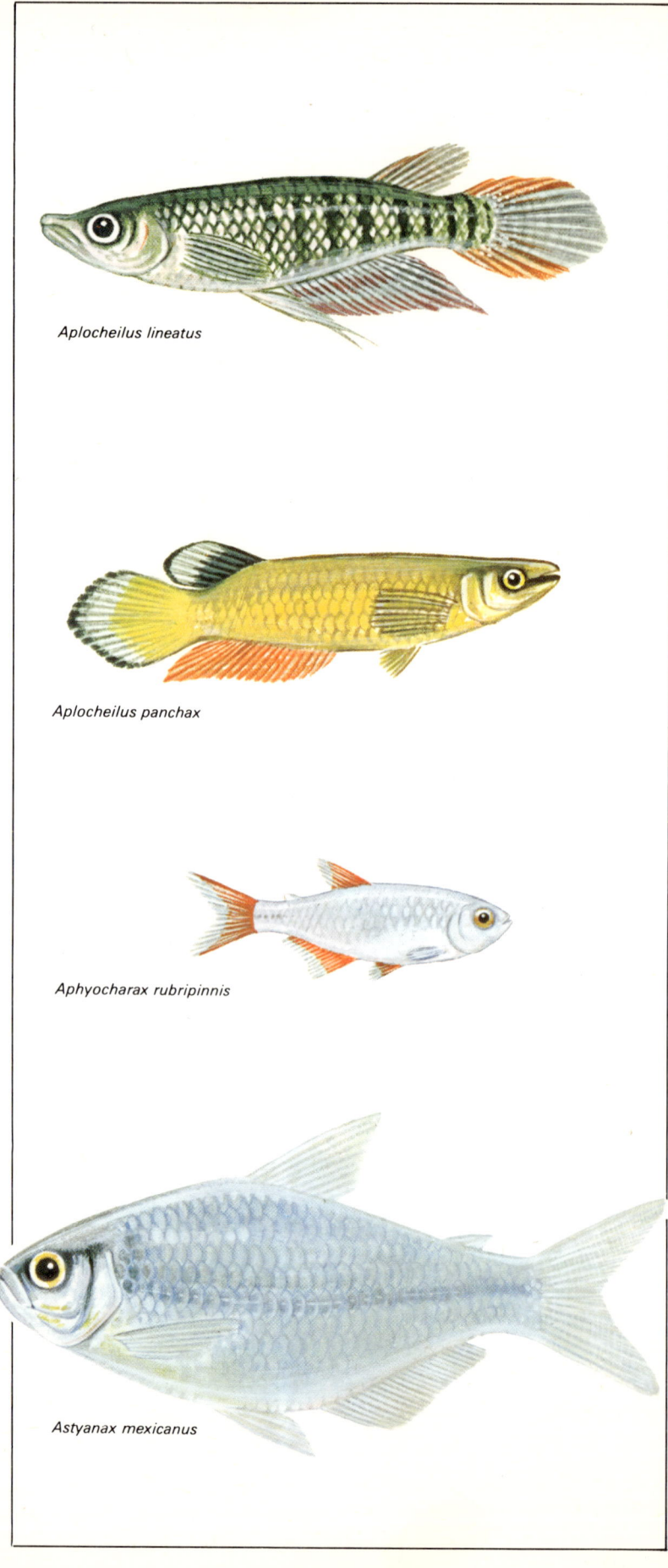

Aplocheilus lineatus

Aplocheilus panchax

Aphyocharax rubripinnis

Astyanax mexicanus

IDENTIFICATION GUIDE

Badis badis

Origin: India, Burma
Reproduction: Oviparous. Will spawn on a piece of slate placed in tank.
Breeding: 77 deg. Male guards the eggs and fry. Female should be removed after spawning. Fry must be fed on infusoria
Average temperature 75 deg. F
Special feeding: Will eat small fish, live foods
Community: Yes. Males become aggressive at breeding time
Size: 3 ins

Barbus conchonius

Common Name: Rosy barb
Origin: India
Reproduction: Oviparous
Breeding: Temperature 75 deg. F Breeding easy
Average temperature 70 deg. F
Special feeding: Will eat most foods
Community: Yes
Size: Grows to 3.5 ins
The male becomes a bright red color at spawning time, thus the common name: Rosy barb.

Barbus everetti

Common Name: Clown barb
Origin: Malaysia
Reproduction: Oviparous
Breeding: Temperature 80 deg. F. Difficult
Average temperature: 75 deg. F
Special feeding: Live foods preferred and will eat vegetable foods and plants, especially *Myriophyllum*
Community: Yes
Size: Grows to 5 ins

Barbus fasciatus

Common Name: Striped barb
Origin: Malaysia
Reproduction: Oviparous
Breeding: Difficult, temperature 78 deg. F, pH 6.5
Average temperature: 75 deg. F
Special feeding: Will eat wide range of food
Community: Yes
Size: 5 ins

Badis badis

Barbus conchonius ♂

♀

Barbus everetti

Barbus fasciatus

IDENTIFICATION GUIDE

Barbus filamentosus

Common Name: Filament barb
Origin: S.W. India
Reproduction: Oviparous
Breeding: Large tank required
Average temperature: 75 deg. F
Special feeding: Dried and live foods acceptable
Community: Yes
Size: 6 ins

Barbus filamentosus

Barbus gelius

Common Name: Golden dwarf barb
Origin: India
Reproduction: Oviparous
Breeding: Temperature 72 deg. F. Eggs hatch in 48 hours
Average temperature: 70 deg. F
Special feeding: Not fussy feeders
Community: Yes
Size: 1.75 ins

Barbus gelius

Barbus lateristriga

Common Name: Spanner barb
Origin: East Indies, Malaysia, Indonesia
Reproduction: Oviparous
Breeding: Difficult. Temperature 75 deg. – 80 deg. F. Sexing is also difficult
Average temperature: 75 deg. F
Special feeding: Daphnia, live foods
Community: No, except while small
Size: 6 ins

Barbus lateristriga

Barbus nigrofasciatus

Common Name: Black ruby
Origin: Southern Sri Lanka
Reproduction: Oviparous
Breeding: Easy, temperature 75 deg. F
Average temperature: 70 deg. F
Special feeding: No special requirements
Community: Yes
Size: 2 ins

Barbus nigrofasciatus

IDENTIFICATION GUIDE

Barbus oligolepsis

Common Name: Checker barb
Origin: Sumatra
Reproduction: Oviparous
Breeding: Difficult, temperature 79 deg. F
Average temperature: 73 deg. F
Special feeding: No special requirements
Community: Yes
Size: 3 ins

Barbus oligolepsis

Barbus schuberti

Common name: Schubert's Barb, Golden Barb
An American bred species not found in the wild state. Males show a row of black spots not present on females

Barbus schuberti

Barbus semifasciolatus

Common Name: Half-banded barb
Origin: China
Reproduction: Oviparous
Breeding: Easy, temperature 75 deg. F
Average temperature: 75 deg. F
Special feeding: Most foods readily accepted
Community: Yes
Size: 2.5 ins

Barbus semifasciolatus

Barbus stoliczkanus

Common name: Stoliczka's Barb
Origin: Burma
Breeding: Easy at 75 deg. — 79 deg. F
Size: Grows to 2½ ins
An attractive Barb from Burma, easy to maintain

Barbus stoliczkanus

IDENTIFICATION GUIDE

Barbus tetrazona

Common Name: Tiger barb
Origin: Malay peninsula, Borneo, Thailand, Sumatra
Reproduction: Oviparous
Breeding: Temperature 80 deg. F
Average temperature: 75 deg. F
Special feeding: Easy to feed, preferably live foods
Community: Yes. A good shoaling fish
Size: Grows to 2 ins

Barbus tetrazona

Barbus ticto

Common Name: Two-spot barb
Origin: India
Reproduction: Oviparous
Breeding: Temperature 76 deg. F
Average temperature: 73 deg. F
Special feeding: No special requirements
Community: Yes
Size: 3.5 ins

Barbus ticto

Barbus titteya

Common Name: Cherry barb
Origin: Sri Lanka
Reproduction: Oviparous
Breeding: Temperature 78 deg. F, eggs hatch in about 40 hours
Average temperature: 70 deg. F
Special feeding: No special requirements
Community: Yes
Size: 2 ins

Barbus titteya ♂

Barbus titteya ♀

Botia macracanthus

Common name: Clown Loach
Origin: Sumatra, Borneo
Size: Can grow to 12 ins but rarely grow to more than 4 ins in the aquaria. This is still one of the biggest Loaches. Its bright coloring makes it a favorite aquarium fish.

Botia macracanthus

IDENTIFICATION GUIDE

Betta splendens

Common Name: Siamese fighter
Origin: Thailand
Reproduction: Oviparous
Breeding: Bubble nester, temperature 78 deg. – 80 deg. F. Bright lighting preferred
Average temperature: 75 deg. F
Special feeding: Live foods
Community: Yes, but aggressive and should not be mixed with males of the same species
Size: 3 ins

Brachydanio albolineatus

Common name: Pearl danio
Origin: Burma, India, Malaya
Reproduction: Oviparous
Breeding: Temperature 75 deg. – 78 deg. F. Easy to breed. Eggs hatch in 48 hours
Average temperature: 75 deg. F
Special feeding: No special requirements
Community: Yes
Size: 2.5 ins

Brachydanio frankei

Common Name: Leopard Danio
Origin: India
Reproduction: Oviparous
Breeding: Temperature 77 deg. F
Average temperature: 75 deg. F
Special feeding: No special requirements
Community: Yes
Size: 2.5 ins

Betta splendens

Brachydanio albolineatus

Brachydanio frankei

IDENTIFICATION GUIDE

Brachydanio rerio

Common Name: Zebra danio
Origin: India
Reproduction: Oviparous
Breeding: Temperature 75 deg. F. A hardy fish more easily spawned than Brachydanio nigrofasciatus
Average temperature: 70 deg. F
Special feeding: No special requirements
Community: Yes
Size: 2 ins

Brachydanio rerio

Brachydanio nigrofasciatus

Common Name: Spotted danio
Origin: Burma
Reproduction: Oviparous
Breeding: Eggs are non adhesive, readily eaten by female. Spawning difficult, hatch in 48 hours
Average temperature: 75 deg. F
Special feeding: No special requirements
Community: Yes
Size: 1.5 ins

Brachydanio nigrofasciatus

Carnegiella strigata

Common Name: Marbled hatchet fish, Flying characin
Origin: Amazon, Guyana
Reproduction: Oviparous
Breeding: Temperature 80 deg. F plus. Well planted tank
Average temperature: 75 deg. F
Community: Yes
Size: 2 ins
In their natural habitat, they swim at high speed close to the surface, searching for food and insects.

Carnegiella strigata

Callichthys callichthys

Common Name: Armored catfish
Origin: S. America
Reproduction: Oviparous
Breeding: Bubble nester among floating plants
Average temperature: 75 deg. F pH 7.2
Special feeding: A good scavenger
Community: Yes
Size: 7 ins

Callichthys callichthys

IDENTIFICATION GUIDE

Brachygobius xanthozonus

Common Name: Bumble-bee goby
Origin: Sumatra, Java and Borneo
Reproduction: Oviparous
Breeding: Temperature 85 deg. F
Average temperature: 77 deg. F
Special feeding: Carnivorous
Community: No. Brackish-water fish
Size: 1.5 ins

Brachygobius xanthozonus

Chanda ranga

Common Name: Indian Glassfish
Origin: India
Reproduction: Oviparous
Breeding: Temperature 76 deg. F
Average temperature: 70 deg. F
Special feeding: Carnivorous, will accept whiteworms and chopped earthworms
Community: Yes. Peaceful, shy fish
Size: 2.5 ins

Chanda ranga

Cheirodon axelrodi

Common name: Cardinal Tetra
Origin: Rio Negro
Size: Grows to 1½ ins
A brilliantly colored fish which looks best in small shoals. Females have a somewhat deeper belly. It is similar to the Neon tetra but grows larger and is more brightly colored. Soft water is essential if eggs are to hatch. Will readily consume most small food

Cheirodon axelrodi

Cichlasoma biocellatum

Common Name: Jack Dempsey
Origin: South America
Reproduction: Oviparous
Breeding: Easy. Temperature 77 deg. F. Eggs deposited on stones
Average temperature: 75 deg. F
Special feeding: Live foods
Community: No
Size: 7 ins

Cichlasoma biocellatum

IDENTIFICATION GUIDE

Cichlasoma festivum

Common Name: Festive cichlid. Flag Chanchito
Origin: Amazon. Guyana
Reproduction: Oviparous
Breeding: Temperature 77 deg. F. Eggs deposited on stones
Average temperature: 75 deg. F
Special feeding: Live foods
Community: Yes. Timid and peaceful, require hiding places.
Size: 6 ins

Cichlasoma festivum

Cichlasoma meeki

Common name: Firemouth cichlid
Origin: Yucatan, Guatemala
Reproduction: Oviparous
Breeding: Temperature 78 deg. F
Average temperature: 75 deg. F
Special feeding: Live foods
Community: No
Size: 5 ins

Cichlasoma meeki

Cichlasoma nigrofasciatum

Common Name: Zebra cichlid. Convict Fish
Origin: Central and South America
Reproduction: Oviparous
Breeding: Temperature 77 deg. F. Builds nest in sand
Average temperature: 75 deg. F
Special feeding: Live foods
Community: No, aggressive
Size: 4 ins

Cichlasoma nigrofasciatum

Cichlasoma severum

Common Name: Striped cichlid, Sedate Chanchito
Origin: South America. Guyana
Reproduction: Oviparous
Breeding: Temperature 80 deg. F
Average temperature: 75 deg. F
Special feeding: Live foods
Community: No, except small species
Size: 7 ins

Cichlasoma severum

IDENTIFICATION GUIDE

Colisa chuna

Common name: Honey dwarf gourami
Origin: India
Reproduction: Oviparous
Breeding: Temperature 82 deg. F. Bubble nest builder
Average temperature: 75 deg. F
Special feeding: Live foods
Community: Yes, but provide cover
Size: 2.5 ins

Colisa fasciata

Common Name: Giant gourami, Striped gourami
Origin: India, Burma
Reproduction: Oviparous
Breeding: Temperature 82 deg. F Bubble nest builder
Average temperature: 75 deg. F
Special feeding: Live foods
Community: Yes, provide cover
Size: 4.5 ins

Colisa labiosa

Common name: Thick-lipped gourami
Origin: Burma
Reproduction: Oviparous
Breeding: Bubble nester. Temperature 80 deg. F
Average temperature: 76 deg. F
Special feeding: Live foods
Community: Yes
Size: 3 ins

Copeina arnoldi

Common Name: Splashing tetra
Origin: Brazil. Amazon Basin
Reproduction: Oviparous
Breeding: Temperature 75 deg. – 80 deg. F pH 7 Lays eggs on leaves above the water surface by jumping up onto them. Provide suitable large-leaved plants. Eggs hatch after 3 – 4 days. The male splashes the eggs from time to time by lashing with its tail
Average temperature: 75 deg. F
Community: Yes
Size: 2 ins

Colisa chuna ♂
Colisa chuna ♀
Colisa fasciata
Colisa labiosa
Copeina arnoldi

IDENTIFICATION GUIDE

Colisa lalia

Common Name: Dwarf gourami
Origin: N. India
Reproduction: Oviparous
Breeding: Bubble nester. Temperature 76 deg. F
Average temperature: 72 deg. F
Special feeding: Live foods
Community: Yes. Provide cover
Size: 2 ins

Copeina guttata

Common Name: Red spotted copeina
Origin: Amazon
Reproduction: Oviparous
Breeding: Easy. Temperature 75 deg. F. Lays eggs in a depression in the sand. Up to 1,000 at one spawning. The male guards the eggs, fanning them with his fins.
Average temperature: 75 deg. F
Special feeding: Live foods preferred
Community, Yes
Size: 3 ins

Corydorus aeneus

Common Name: Bronze catfish
Origin: West Indies. South America
Reproduction: Oviparous. Adhesive eggs
Breeding: Temperature 78 deg. F
Average temperature: 75 deg. F pH 7.2
Special feeding: A good scavenger
Community: Yes
Size: 3 ins

Corydorus hastatus

Common Name: Dwarf catfish. Pygmy catfish
Origin: S. America. Amazon Basin
Reproduction: Oviparous. Eggs laid on stones, hatch in 3–4 days. Parents liable to eat fry
Breeding: Temperature 80 deg. F
Average temperature: 76 deg. F pH 7.2
Special feeding: A good scavenger
Community: Yes
Size: 1.75 ins

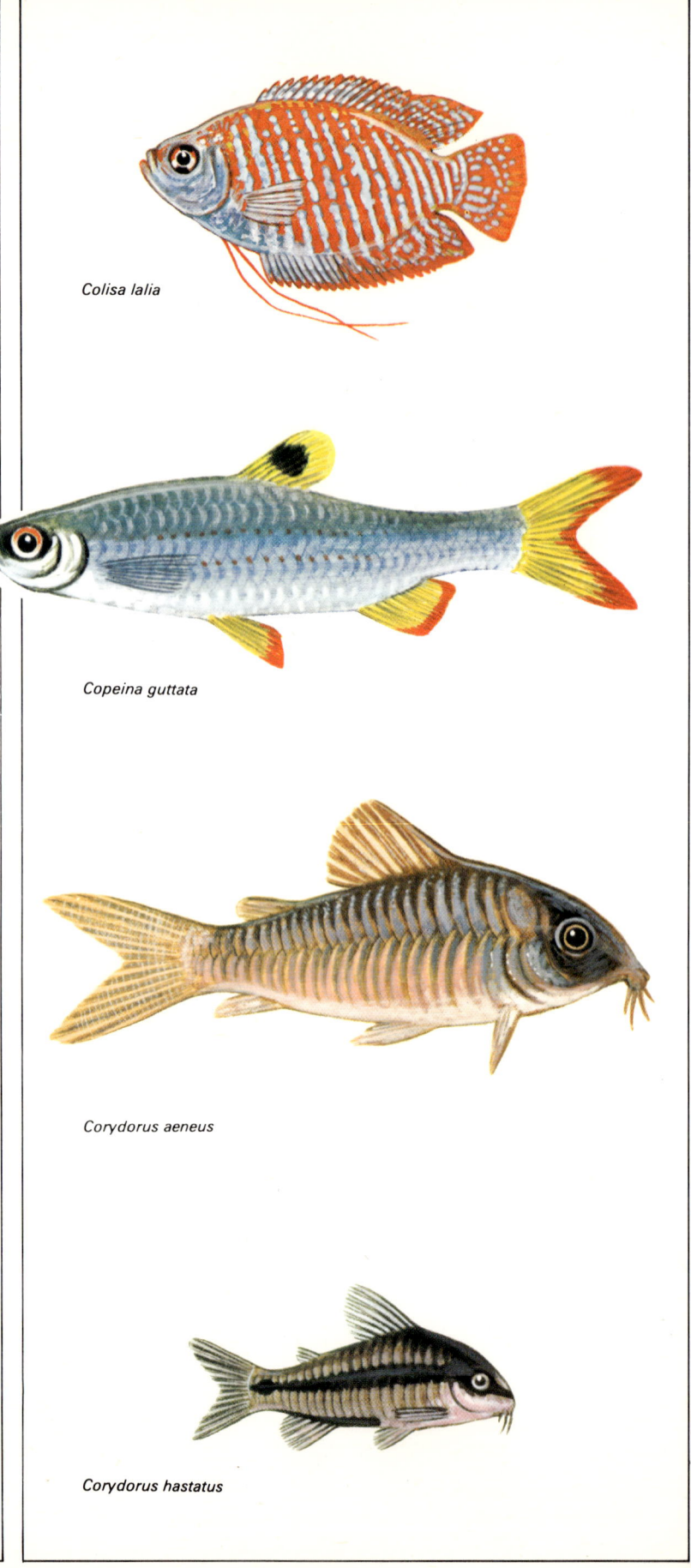

Colisa lalia

Copeina guttata

Corydorus aeneus

Corydorus hastatus

IDENTIFICATION GUIDE

Corydorus nattereri

Common Name: Blue catfish
Origin: Brazil
Reproduction: Oviparous
Breeding: Temperature 79 deg. F
Average temperature: 77 deg. F
pH 7.2
Special feeding: Live foods
Community: Yes
Size: 2.5 ins

Corydorus julii

Common Name: Leopard catfish
Origin: Brazil
Reproduction: Oviparous
Breeding: Temperature 80 deg. F
Average temperature: 78 deg. F
pH 7.2
Special feeding: Live foods
Community: Yes
Size: 2.5 ins

Corydorus paleatus

Common Name: Peppered catfish
Origin: Argentine, Brazil
Reproduction: Oviparous
Breeding: 76 deg. F
Average temperature: 70 deg. F
Special feeding: Live foods
Community: Yes
Size: 3 ins

Corynopoma riisei

Common Name: Swordtail characin
Origin: S. America, W. Indies, Venezuela
Reproduction: Oviparous
Breeding: Temperature 79 deg. F.
Average temperature: 76 deg. F
Special feeding: Will eat most foods
Community: Yes
Size: 2 ins

Ctenopoma fasciolatum

Common name: Banded Climbing Perch
Origin: Congo Basin
Average temperature: 75 deg. F
Special feeding: Live foods, small fish
Community: No
Size: Grows to 3 ins

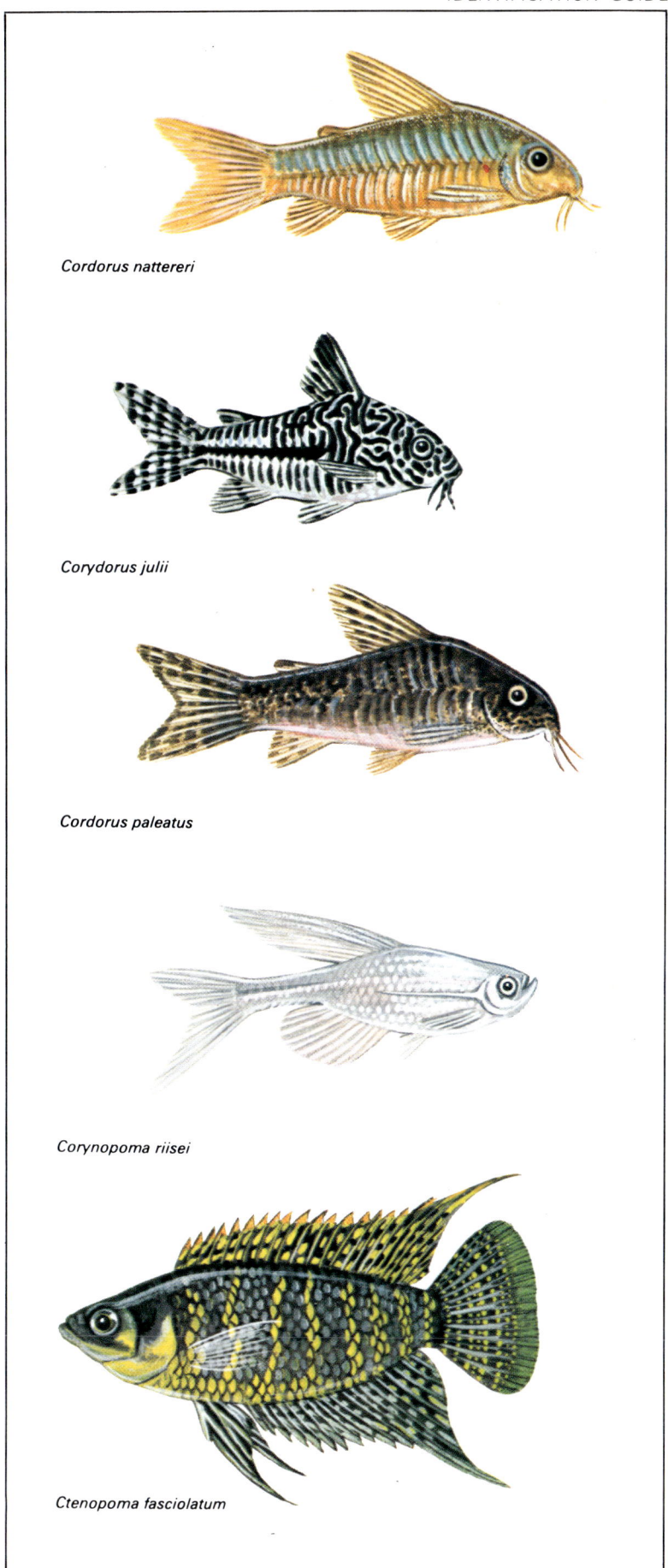

Cordorus nattereri

Corydorus julii

Cordorus paleatus

Corynopoma riisei

Ctenopoma fasciolatum

IDENTIFICATION GUIDE

Ctenobrycon spilurus

Common Name: Silver tetra
Origin: S. America
Reproduction: Oviparous
Breeding: Temperature 75 deg. – 80 deg. F. Lays adhesive eggs on plants. Up to 800, hatching in about 48 hours
Average temperature: 70 deg. F
Special feeding: Omnivorous. Algae and other green foods
Community: Yes
Size: 3 ins

Cynolebias bellottii

Common Name: Argentine Pearl Fish, Blue chromide
Origin: Brazil
Reproduction: Oviparous
Breeding: Temperature 72 deg. F. Breeding extremely difficult. After spawning the fish should be removed and the water syphoned off leaving ground cover to almost dry out. After 3 weeks the aquarium water should be replaced. Fry hatch after 6 – 8 weeks
Average temperature: 70 deg. F
Special feeding: Live foods
Community: No, best kept with own species
Size: 3 ins

Danio devario

Common Name: Bengal danio
Origin: N.W. India
Reproduction: Oviparous
Breeding: Usual for Danios
Average temperature: 75 deg. F
Special feeding: No special requirements
Community: Yes
Size: 4 ins

Danio malabaricus

Common Name: Giant danio
Origin: India, Malabar, Sri Lanka
Reproduction: Oviparous
Breeding: Easy. Temperature 80 deg. F. Eggs are adhesive
Average temperature: 72 deg. F
Special feeding: Live foods
Community: Yes, with fish of similar size
Size: 5 ins

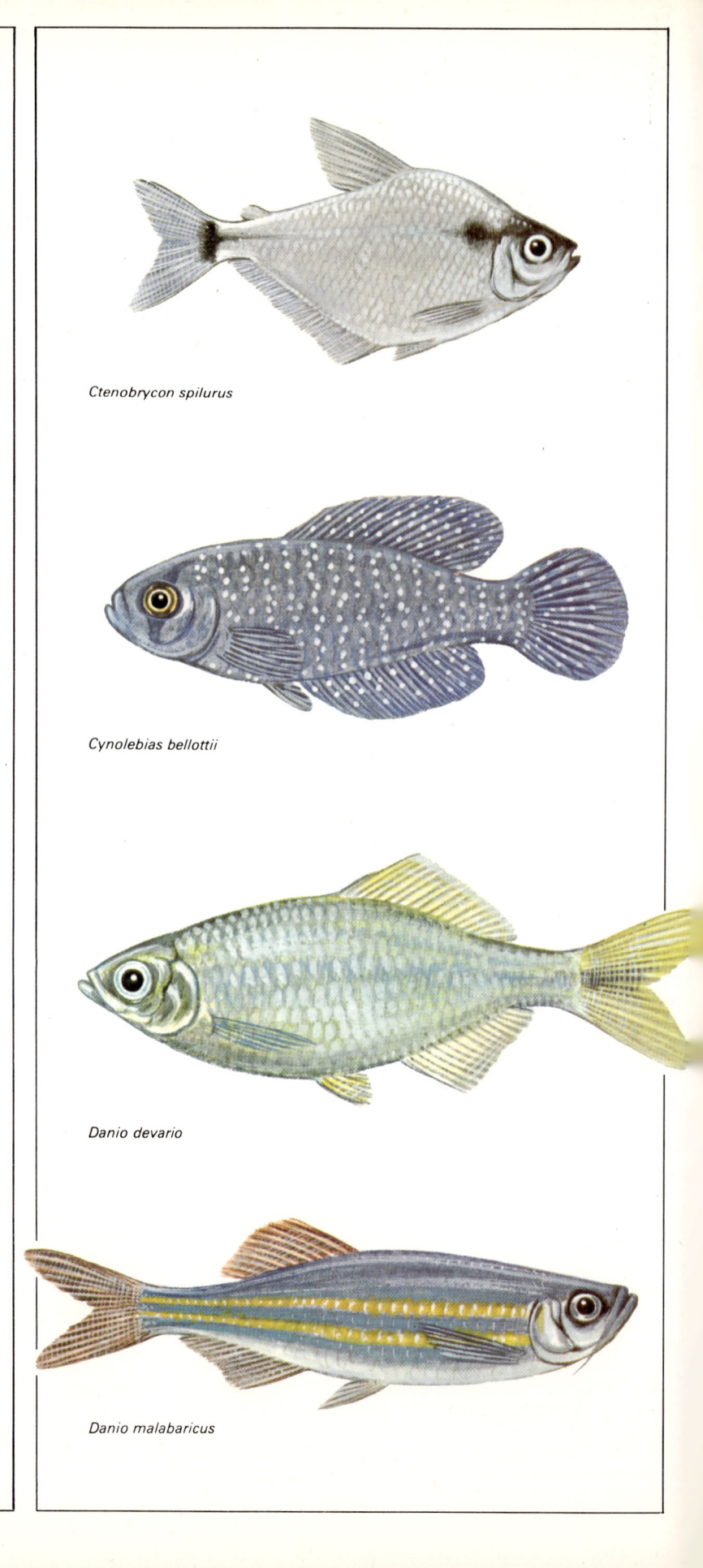

Ctenobrycon spilurus

Cynolebias bellottii

Danio devario

Danio malabaricus

IDENTIFICATION GUIDE

Elassoma evergladei

Common Name: Pigmy sunfish
Origin: Florida, North Carolina
Breeding: Oviparous. Temperature 66 deg. F pH 4.0 to 5.0 Builds a nest of fine-leaved plants near the bottom. Eggs hatch in 48 hours
Average temperature: 64 deg. F
Special feeding: Carnivorous. Must have live food
Community, Yes
Size: 1.25 ins

Elassoma evergladei

Epalzeorhynchus kallopterus

Common name: Flying Fox
Origin: Sumatra, Borneo
Community: Yes, but must not be kept with other specimens of its own kind
Size: Grows to 3½ ins

Epalzeorhynchus kallopterus

Epiplatys dageti

Common Name: Fire-mouth Killie
Origin: West Africa
Reproduction: Oviparous
Breeding: Temperature 76 deg. F. Eggs are deposited on plants over a period of 2 – 3 weeks. Fry hatch in 1 – 3 weeks
Average temperature: 72 deg. F pH 6.5
Special feeding: Live foods
Community: Yes
Size: 2.25 ins

Epiplatys dageti

Etroplus maculatus

Common Name: Orange chromide
Origin: India and Sri Lanka
Reproduction: Oviparous
Breeding: Temperature 84 deg. F
Average temperature: 75 deg. F
Special feeding: Live foods
Community: Yes
Size: 3 ins

Etroplus maculatus

IDENTIFICATION GUIDE

Gasteropelecus levis

Common Name: Hatchet fish
Origin: Guyana, Amazon Basin
Reproduction: Oviparous
Breeding: Very difficult
Average temperature: 75 deg. F
Special feeding: Carnivorous only. Live foods. Feeding difficult. Surface feeders
Community: Yes
Size: 2.25 ins

This is a difficult fish to keep in captivity. Because of their finnicky diet, they seldom survive for very long. Liable to jump out of uncovered aquaria.

Gasteropelecus levis

Gymnocorymbus ternetzi

Common Name: Black widow, Black tetra
Origin: Paraguay
Reproduction: Oviparous
Breeding: Temperature 80 deg. F
Average temperature: 70 deg. F
Special feeding: Omnivorous
Community: Yes
Size: 2.5 ins

Gymnocorymbus ternetzi

Hasemania marginata

Common name: Copper Tetra, Silver Tipped Tetra
Origin: South-eastern Brazil
Average temperature: 68 deg. – 75 deg. F
Special feeding: As other tetras, feed fry with infusorians or sieved hard-boiled yolk of egg
Community: Yes
Size: Grows to 1½ ins. Female larger and paler than the male Often confused with *Hemigrammus nanus*
Note that *Hasemania marginata* has no adipose fin

Hasemania marginata

Haplochromis multicolor

Common Name: Egyptian mouthbreeder
Origin: Egypt, E. Africa
Reproduction: Oviparous
Breeding: Temperature 77 deg. F, easy to breed
Average temperature: 72 deg. F
Special feeding: Live foods
Community: No
Size: 3 ins

Haplochromis multicolor

IDENTIFICATION GUIDE

Helostoma temmincki

Common Name: Kissing gourami
Origin: Borneo, Thailand, Sumatra, India.
Reproduction: Oviparous
Breeding: Egg scatterer. Temperature 85 deg. F pH 7.5 difficult
Average temperature: 75 deg. F
Special feeding: Algae, spinach, lettuce
Community: No
Size: 5 – 12 ins

Helostoma temmincki

Hemichromis bimaculatus

Common Name: Jewel cichlid
Origin: Africa
Reproduction: Oviparous
Breeding: Temperature 77 deg. F. Breed as Cichlids
Special feeding: Live foods
Community: No, aggressive
Size: 5 ins

Hemichromis bimaculatus

Hemigrammus caudovittatus

Common Name: Brazilian tetra. Buenos Aires tetra
Origin: La Plata Basin
Reproduction: Oviparous
Breeding: Temperature 73 deg. F. Lays eggs among plants
Average temperature: 70 deg. F
Special feeding: carefully selected, small live food
Community: Yes. Females more aggressive than males
Size: 3 ins

Hemigrammus caudovittatus

Hemigrammus armstrongi

Common name: Golden Tetra
Origin: Western Guyana
Breeding: Easy
Size: Grows to 1¾ ins
An easily-bred fish which is an attractive golden color when young

Hemigrammus armstrongi

Hemigrammus erythrozonus

Common name: Glowlight Tetra
Origin: Guyana
Average temperature: 75 deg. F
Breeding: Temperature 82 deg. F
Size: Grows to 1¾ ins

Hemigrammus erythrozonus

IDENTIFICATION GUIDE

Hemigrammus nanus

Common name: Silver-tipped Tetra
Origin: Rio San Francisco, Eastern Brazil
Size: 2 ins
Often confused with *Hasemania marginata*
The tail base marking of this tetra is darker than that of *Hasemania marginata* and it has the adipose fin

Hemigrammus ocellifer

Common Name: Head and Tail-light tetra
Origin: Amazon Basin, Guyana
Reproduction: Oviparous
Breeding: Temperature 75 deg. F. Easy
Average temperature: 72 deg. F
Special feeding: Small, live food
Community: Yes
Size: 1.75 ins

Hemigrammus rhodostomus

Common Name: Red-nosed tetra
Origin: Lower Amazon
Reproduction: Oviparous
Breeding: Large well planted tank, 10 ins water
Average temperature: 76 deg. F
Special feeding: Small, live food
Community: Yes
Size: 1.5 ins

Hemigrammus unilineatus

Common Name: Feather fin
Origin: S. America
Reproduction: Oviparous
Breeding: Temperature 75–77 deg. F
Average temperature: 75 deg. F
Special feeding: Small, live food
Community: Yes
Size: 2.5 ins

Hemigrammus nanus

Hemigrammus ocellifer

Hemigrammus rhodostomus

Hemigrammus unilineatus

IDENTIFICATION GUIDE

Heterandria formosa

Common Name: Mosquito fish, Pygmy live-bearer, Dwarf top minnow
Origin: N. Carolina to Florida
Reproduction: Viviparous. Young delivered at the rate of 2 or 3 a day during a period of about 10 days
Breeding: Temperature 78 deg. F
Average temperature: 73 deg. F
Special feeding: Small live food
Community: No. Due to their small size they are best kept only with their own kind. Otherwise a peaceful fish
Size: Less than an inch long

Heterandria formosa ♀
♂

Hyphessobrycon eos

Common Name: Dawn tetra
Origin: Guyana
Reproduction: Oviparous
Breeding: Difficult. Temperature 75 – 78 deg. F
Average temperature: 75 deg. F
Special feeding: Small, live food
Community: Yes
Size: 2 ins

Hyphessobrycon eos

Hyphessobrycon flammeus

Common name: Flame fish
Origin: Brazil
Reproduction: Oviparous
Breeding: Easy. Temperature 72 – 75 deg. F. Eggs layed among plants. Eggs hatch in 48 hours
Average temperature: 70 deg. F
Size: 1.5 ins

Hyphessobrycon flammeus

Hyphessobrycon heterorhabdus

Common Name: Flag tetra
Origin: Amazon
Reproduction: Oviparous
Breeding: Difficult
Average temperature: 75 deg. F
Special feeding: Live food
Community: Yes, with similar sized fish
Size: 2 ins

Hyphessobrycon heterorhabdus

IDENTIFICATION GUIDE

Hyphessobrycon innesi

Common Name: Neon tetra
Origin: Amazon
Reproduction: Oviparous
Breeding: Difficult. Temperature 75 deg. F pH 6.5 Feed fry on egg yolk suspended in muslin bag
Average temperature: 72 deg. F
Special feeding: Small live food
Community: Yes, with fish of similar size
Size: 1.5 ins

Hyphessobrycon innesi

Hyphessobrycon metae

Common name: Loreto Tetra
Origin: Meta Riva, South America
Size: Grows to 1.75 in

Hyphessobrycon metae

Hyphessobrycon ornatus

Common Name: Ornate tetra
Origin: South America
Reproduction: Oviparous
Breeding: Temperature 80 deg. F
Average temperature: 76 deg. F
Special feeding: Small, live food
Community: Yes
Size: 1.5 ins

Hyphessobrycon ornatus

Hyphessobrycon pulchripinnis

Common Name: Lemon tetra
Origin: Amazon Basin
Reproduction: Oviparous
Breeding: Temperature 80 deg. F. pH 7.2 – 7.4 Difficult
Average temperature: 73 deg. F
Special feeding: Live food
Community: Yes
Size: 1.5 ins

Hyphessobrycon pulchripinnis

46

IDENTIFICATION GUIDE

Hyphessobrycon rosaceus

Common name: Rosy tetra
Origin: Guyana and Brazil
Reproduction: Oviparous
Breeding: Difficult. Temperature 80 deg. F
Average temperature, 75 deg. F
Special feeding: Live food
Community: Yes, with small fish
Size: 1.75 ins

Hyphessobrycon rosaceus

Hyphessobrycon scholzei

Common name: Black-line tetra
Origin: Amazon
Reproduction: Oviparous
Breeding: Easy. Temperature 78 deg. F
Special feeding: Live food
Community: No, aggressive
Size: 2 ins

Hyphessobrycon scholzei

Hyphessobrycon serpae

Origin: Brazil
Reproduction: Oviparous
Breeding: Difficult. Temperature 80 deg. F
Average temperature: 76 deg. F
Special feeding: Live food
Community: Yes
Size: 1.5 ins

Hyphessobrycon serpae

Jordanella floridae

Common Name: Flag fish
Origin: Florida
Reproduction: Oviparous
Breeding: Temperature 75 deg. F. Remove female after spawning. Male protects eggs
Average Temperature: 70 deg. F pH 6.5
Special feeding: Vegetarian: Algae, spinach, lettuce (frozen then thawed)
Community: Yes, with similar sized fish, but somewhat aggressive
Size: 2.25 ins

Jordanella floridae

IDENTIFICATION GUIDE

Kryptopterus bicirris

Common name: Glass Catfish
Origin: Indonesia, South East Asia
Average temperature: 68 deg. — 77 deg. F
Special feeding: Prefers live food no special feeding
Community: Yes
Size: Grows to 4 ins
The origin of the common name is immediately apparent since the body is almost entirely transparent.

Labeo bicolor

Common Name: Red-tailed black shark
Origin: Thailand
Reproduction: Oviparous
Breeding: Moderately easy
Average temperature: 75 deg. F
Special feeding: Live food
Community: Yes. A timid fish despite its name. Hiding places required. More than a pair of this species tend to be quarrelsome
Size: 5 ins

Lebistes reticulatus

Common Name: Guppy, Rainbow fish
Origin: Trinidad, Venezuela
Reproduction: Viviporous
Breeding: Prolific breeder, from 5—60 young. Temperature 76 deg. F
Average temperature: 70 deg. F
Special feeding: Frequent feeding necessary
Community: Yes
Size: Males to 1.5 ins, females to 2.25 ins

Limia nigrofasciata

Common Name: Black Barred Limia, Hump-Back Limia
Origin: Haiti
Reproduction: Viviparous
Breeding: Temperature 78 deg. F
Average temperature: 75 deg. F
Special feeding: Omnivorous
Community: Yes
Size: Males 2 ins, females 2.5 ins

Kryptopterus bicirris

Labeo bicolor

Lebistes reticulatus

Limia nigrofasciata

IDENTIFICATION GUIDE

Limia melanogaster

Common Name: Blue limia
Origin: Jamaica
Reproduction: Viviparous
Breeding: Temperature 78 deg. F
Average temperature: 75 deg. F
Special feeding: Omnivorous
Community: Yes
Size: 2.5 ins

Limia melanogaster

Macropodus cupanus dayi

Common name: Brown spike-tailed Paradise Fish
Origin: Burma, South Vietnam, Southern India
Reproduction: Oviparous
Average temperature: 70 deg. F
Breeding temperature: 70 to 77 deg. F
Male can be distinguished by slightly longer fins than the female
Size: Grows to 3 ins

Macropodus cupanus dayi

Macropodus opercularis

Common name: Paradise fish
Origin: China, Korea, Taiwan
Reproduction: Oviparous
Breeding: Temperature 75 deg. F Bubble nester
Average temperature: 70 deg. F
Special feeding: Live foods
Community: No
Size: 3 ins

Macropodus opercularis

Megalamphodus megalopterus

Common Name: Black phantom tetra
Origin: Brazil
Reproduction: Oviparous
Breeding: Large, well planted aquarium
Average temperature: 75 deg. F
Special feeding: Will accept most foods
Community: Yes
Size: 1.5 ins

Megalamphodus megalopterus

IDENTIFICATION GUIDE

Moenkhausia pittieri

Common Name: Diamond tetra
Origin: Venezuela (Lake Valencia)
Reproduction: Oviparous
Breeding: Difficult. Temperature 78 deg. F
Average temperature: 73 deg. F
Special feeding: Omnivorous. Has a tendency to eat plants
Community: Yes
Size: 2.5 ins

Monodactylus argenteus

Common Name: Malayan angelfish
Origin: Malaysia, E. Africa, N. Australia
Reproduction: Oviparous
Breeding: Little known
Average temperature: 75 deg. F Brackish water fish
Special feeding: Plant food essential part of diet
Community, Yes
Size: 5 ins

Nannaethiops unitaeniatus

Common Name: African tetra
Origin: Ghana, Nile, Congo
Reproduction: Oviparous
Breeding: Temperature 78–80 deg. F. Ready breeder, depositing eggs among fine-leaved plants. Eggs hatch in 48 hours
Average temperature: 73 deg. F
Special feeding: Omnivorous
Community: Yes
Size: Males 2.5 ins, females 3 ins

Nannacara anomala

Common Name: Golden-eyed dwarf cichlid
Origin: Guyana
Reproduction: Oviparous
Breeding: Temperature 80 deg. F
Average temperature: 76 deg. F
Special feeding: Live foods
Community: Yes
Size: 2.75 ins

Moenkhausia pittieri

Monodactylus argenteus

Nannaethiops unitaeniatus

Nannacara anomala

IDENTIFICATION GUIDE

Nannostomus marginatus

Common name: Dwarf pencil-fish
Origin: S. America, Amazon, Guyana
Reproduction: Oviparous
Breeding: Temperature 80 deg. F pH 6.5. Difficult
Average temperature: 75 deg. F
Special feeding: Omnivorous. Due to their small mouths food needs to be carefully selected
Community: Yes
Size: 1.25 ins

Nannostomus trifasciatus

Origin: Amazon
Reproduction: Oviparous
Breeding: Difficult. Temperature 75 deg. F. Eggs hatch in 2–3 days
Average temperature: 75 deg. F
Special feeding: Due to their small mouths, small food should be given
Community: Yes
Size: 1.75 ins
When startled, the stripes become paler

Nematobrycon palmeri

Common Name: Emperor tetra
Origin: Colombia
Reproduction: Oviparous
Breeding: Temperature 80 deg. F
Average temperature: 77 deg. F
Special feeding: Will accept most foods
Community: Yes, a shy fish
Size: 2.5 ins

Nothobranchius guentheri

Common Name: E. African Killifish
Origin: E. Africa
Reproduction: Oviparous
Breeding: Egg burier. After spawning, remove fish, drain tank for 12 weeks, refill and await hatching
Average temperature: 75 deg. F
Special feeding: Live foods
Community: No
Size: Female 1.5 ins, male 1.75 ins

Nannostomus marginatus

Nannostomus trifasciatus

Nematobrycon palmeri

Nothobranchius guentheri

IDENTIFICATION GUIDE

Pachypanchax playfairii

Common Name: Playfairs panchax
Origin: Seychelles. E. Africa
Reproduction: Oviparous. Eggs attached to roots of floating plants. Well planted tank. Adults will eat eggs. Temperature 77 deg. F
Average temperature: 75 deg. F A teaspoonful of salt to each gallon of water is beneficial
Special feeding: Carnivorous. Live food
Community: No
Size: 4 ins
The scales of this species should stand out from the body, this is quite normal.

Pterolebias peruensis

Origin: Peru
Average temperature: 70 deg. — 74 deg. F
Size: Grows to 3 ins (male) 2 ins (female)
This fish buries its eggs which hatch after sixteen weeks, if dried out, or up to 28 weeks if kept wet

Poecilia latipinna

Common name: Sailfin Molly
Origin: Eastern USA
Reproduction: Viviparous
Breeding: Easy in well planted tanks
Average temperature: 70 deg. F
Special feeding: Will accept most foods but require algae, lettuce or spinach as essential diet supplement
Community: Yes
Size: Grows to 4 ins

Poecilia formosa

Common name: Lyretail Molly
Origin: Mexico
This species is a natural cross of *P. Latipinna* with *P. sphenops*. and only females are produced. These can be mated with a male from either of the original species
Average temperature: 70 deg. F
Special feeding: Some green food essential
Size: Grows to 3–5 ins

Pachypanchax playfairii

Pterolebias peruensis

Poecilia lattipinna

Poecilia formosa

IDENTIFICATION GUIDE

Poecilia sphenops

Common Name: Short-finned Molly
Origin: N. America
Reproduction: Viviparous
Breeding: Temperature 80 deg. F Alkaline water preferred
Special feeding: Live foods
Community: Yes
Size: 3.5 ins

Poecilia sphenops

Poecilia velifera

Common Name: Giant sail-fin molly
Origin: Yucatan
Reproduction: Viviparous
Breeding: Temperature 80 deg. F Alakaline water preferred. Up to 100 fry to a brood
Average temperature: 75 deg. F
Special feeding: Live food
Community: Yes
Size: 5 ins

Poecilia velifera

Pristella riddlei

Common name: X-ray Tetra
Origin: S. America
Average temperature: 75 deg. F
Special feeding: Will accept most foods of small size
Community: Yes
Size: Grows to 2 ins
Good community fish

Pristella riddlei

Pyrrhulina vittata

Common name: Striped Vittata
Origin: Amazon region
Size: Grows to 2 ins
Feeding: Most food accepted
A peaceful, delicate fish
Lives close to the surface and deposits eggs on broad leaved plants which are first carefully cleaned by the male

Pyrrhulina vittata

53

IDENTIFICATION GUIDE

Pseudocorynopoma doriae

Common name: Dragon-Finned Characin
Origin: South Brazil and La Plata district
Average temperature: 60 deg. — 64 deg. F
Size: Grows to 3 ins

Pseudocorynopoma doriae

Pseudotropheus auratus

Common Name: Golden Lake Nyasa Cichlid
Origin: Lake Nyasa, Africa
Reproduction: Oviparous
Breeding: pH 7.5 — 8 Eggs laid in depression dug by male
Average temperature: 75 deg. F
Special feeding: Live foods, algae, spinach
Community: No. Male is aggressive to female. Cover should be provided. Initially, male and female should be separated by glass partition until acclimatized
Size: 4 ins

♀

♂

Pseudotropheus auratus

Pterophyllum scalare

Common Name, Angel fish
Origin: Amazon
Reproduction: Oviparous
Breeding: Temperature 80 deg. F. Up to 1,000 eggs laid in neat rows on rocks over a small area, during a 2 hour spawning period. The female fans the eggs while the male stands guard. If allowed to raise young, an average brood of 50 can be expected
Average temperature: 77 deg. F pH lower than 7.8
Special feeding: Does best on live foods
Community: Yes, while small
Size, 5 ins

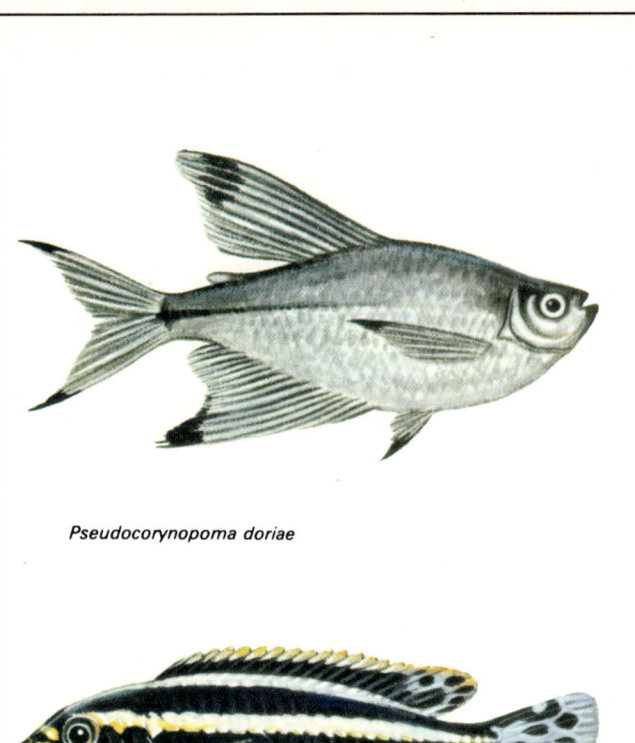

Pterophyllum scalare

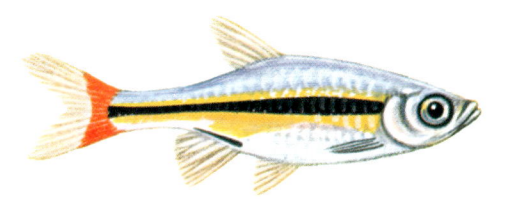

IDENTIFICATION GUIDE

Rasbora borapetensis

Rasbora elegans

Rasbora heteromorpha

Rasbora borapetensis

Common Name: Red-tailed Rasbora
Origin: Thailand
Reproduction: Oviparous. Adhesive eggs. Temperature 82 deg. F pH 6.5
Average temperature: 77 deg. F
Special feeding, No special requirements, although live food preferred
Community: Yes
Size: 2.5 ins

Rasbora elegans

Common Name: Two-spot Rasbora
Origin: Malay Peninsular
Reproduction: Oviparous. Adhesive eggs. Temperature 82 deg. F pH 6.5
Average temperature: 77 deg. F
Special feeding: Live food
Community: Yes
Size: 5 ins

Rasbora heteromorpha

Common Name: Harlequin
Origin: Sumatra
Reproduction: Oviparous
Breeding: Very difficult. Temperature 80 deg. F pH 6.5 Sexing difficult
Average temperature: 75 deg. F
Special feeding: Live food an essential part of diet
Community: Yes
Size: 2.5 ins
Provide broad leaved plants e.g. *Cryptocoryne*. If spawning takes place the parents should be removed as they will eat the eggs. Males slightly brighter.

IDENTIFICATION GUIDE

Rasbora maculata

Common Name: Dwarf rasbora, Spotted rasbora
Origin: Malaysia, Indo China, Malacca
Reproduction: Oviparous
Breeding: 80 deg. F pH 6.3 Feed fry egg yolk emulsion. see *R. heteromorpha*
Average temperature: 76 deg. F
Special feeding: Living food an essential part of diet
Community: Yes, but not with much larger fish
Size: 1 in

Rasbora maculata

Rasbora pauciperforata

Common Name: Red-striped Rasbora
Origin: Malay Peninsula
Reproduction: Oviparous
Breeding: Soft water preferred
Average temperature: 77 deg. F
Special feeding: Live foods
Community: Yes
Size: 2.5 ins

Rasbora pauciperforata

Rasbora trilineata

Common Name: Scissor-tail
Origin: Malay peninsular
Reproduction: Oviparous
Breeding: Temperature 80 deg. F pH 6.8 see *R. heteromorpha*
Average temperatre: 75 deg. F
Special feeding: Living food an essential part of diet
Community: Yes
Size, 3 ins

Rasbora trilineata

Rivulus cylindraceus

Common Name: Green Rivulus
Origin: Cuba, Florida
Reproduction: Oviparous
Breeding: Temperature 77 deg. F. Eggs are scattered among thick plants. Hatch in about 12 — 14 days
Average temperature: 75 deg. F
Special feeding: Live foods, insects
Community: Yes
Size: 2 ins

♂
♀

Rivulus cylindraceus

IDENTIFICATION GUIDE

Scatophagus argus

Common Name: Spotted scat
Origin: East Indies
Breeding: Little known. Brackish water fish
Average temperature: 74 deg. F
Special feeding: Will eat most foods
Community: Yes. Peaceful, but aggressive feeders. Will crop plants down to the roots.
Size, 4 ins

Symphysoden discus

Common Name: Discus, Red discus
Origin: Amazon
Reproduction: Oviparous
Breeding: Difficult. Temperature 84 deg. F pH 5.5
Average temperature: 78 deg. F pH 6.2—6.6 Peat filter beneficial
Special feeding: Live foods
Community: No
Size: 5.5 ins

Tanichthys albonubes

Common Name: White Cloud Mountain Minnow
Origin: China
Reproduction: Oviparous
Breeding: Ready breeder. Plant fine-leaved plants e.g. *Mymophyllum*
Average temperature: 68 deg. F pH 7.5
Special feeding: Omnivorous
Community: Yes
Size: 2 ins

Thayeria obliqua

Common Name: Penguin
Origin: Amazon Basin
Reproduction: Oviparous
Breeding: Moderately easy. Eggs deposited on lower leaves of plants, hatch in about 48 hours
Average temperature: 73 deg. F
Special feeding: Fry need algae
Community: Yes
Size: 3 ins
Aquarium should be covered at all times, as this is a very active leaping fish.

Scatophagus argus

Symphysoden discus

Tanichthys albonubes

Thayeria obliqua

IDENTIFICATION GUIDE

Toxotes jaculator

Common name: Archer Fish
Origin: S. Asia, China, India, Australia, Phillipines
Average temperature: 77 deg. – 82 deg. F
Size: Grows to 4 ins

A very interesting fish that has the ability to spit water and uses this technique to shoot down flies and small winged insects. Not a good community fish. Very difficult to feed in captivity. It seems to favor brackish water, and spends much of its time close to the surface

Trichogaster leeri

Common Name: Pearl gourami. Lace gourami
Origin: Thailand, Sumatra, Malaysia
Reproduction: Oviparous
Breeding: Easy. Temperature 80 deg. F
Average temperature: 76 deg. F
pH 6.5
Special feeding: Live foods
Community: Yes
Size: 4 ins

Trichogaster trichopterus

Common Name: Three-spot gourami
Origin: Indo China, Malaysia, Burma, Indonesia
Reproduction: Oviparous
Breeding: Temperature 80 deg. F
Average temperature: 75 deg. F
Special feeding: Live foods
Community: Yes, but aggressive
Size: 5 ins

Trichopsis vittatus

Common Name: Croaking Gourami
Origin: Malaysia, Thailand, S. Vietnam
Reproduction: Oviparous
Breeding: Temperature 85 deg. F
Average temperature: 75 deg. F
Special feeding: Live foods
Community: Yes
Size: 2 ins

Toxotes jaculator

Trichogaster leeri

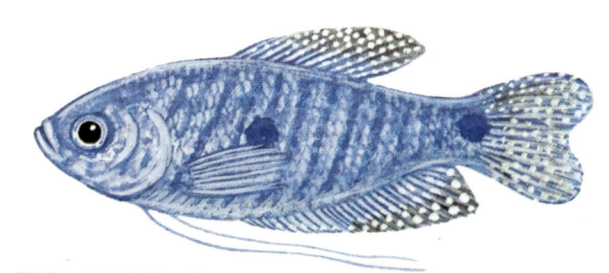

Trichogaster trichopterus

Trichopsis vittatus

IDENTIFICATION GUIDE

Xenomystus Nigri

Common name: African Knife Fish
Origin: Central and Western Africa
Average temperature: 70 deg. — 80 deg. F, preferred water, slightly acid
Special feeding: Most live foods
Community: No
Size: Grows to 8 ins

Xenomystus nigri

Xiphophorus hellerii

Common Name: Swordtail
Origin: E. Mexico
Reproduction: Ovoviviparous 100 — 150 to a single breed
Breeding: Easy. Temperature 78 — 80 deg. F Interesting courtship behavior
Average temperature: 70 deg. F
Special feeding: Algae eaters. Prefer a diet of vegetable and live foods
Community: Yes, but larger fish tend to bully
Size: 3 ins

Xiphophorus hellerii

Xiphophorus maculatus

Common Name: Platy
Origin: E. Mexico, Guatemala
Reproduction: Ovoviviparous
Breeding: Easy. Temperature 78 deg. F
Average temperature: 74 deg. F
Special feeding, Prefer diet of vegetable and live foods
Community: Yes
Size: 1.5 ins

Xiphophorus maculatus

Xiphophorus variatus

Common Name: Variegated platy
Origin: E. Mexico
Reproduction: Ovoviviparous
Breeding: Temperature 78 deg. F
Average temperature: 74 deg. F
Special feeding, Prefer diet of vegetable and live foods
Community: Yes
Size: Female 3 ins, male smaller

Xiphophorus variatus

Index

Anostomus anostomus 26
Aphyosemion australe 26
   bivittatum 26
   coeruleum 26
Apistogramma ramireze 27
Arnoldichthys spilopterus 27
Acanthopthalmus semicintus 27
Aequidens maronii 27
Aplocheilus lineatus 28
   panchax 28
Aphyocharax rubripinnis 28
Astyanax mexicanus 28
Badis badis 29
Barbus conchonius 29
   everetti 29
   fasciatus 29
   filamentosus 30
   gelius 30
   lateristriga 30
   nigrofasciatus 30
   oligolepis 31
   schuberti 31
   semifasciolatus 31
   stoliczkanus 31
   tetrazona 32
   ticto 32
   titteya 32
Betta splendens 33
Botia macracanthus 32
Brachydanio frankei 33
   rerio 34
   nigrofasciatus 34
Brachygobius xanthozonus 35
Callichthys callichthys 34
Carnegiella strigata 34
Chanda ranga 35
Cheirodon axelrodi 35
Cichlasoma biocellatum 35
   festivum 36
   meeki 36
   nigrofasciatum 36
   severum 36
Colisa chuna 37
   fasciata 37
   labiosa 37
   lalia 38
Copeina arnoldi 37
   guttata 38
Corydorus aeneus 38
   hastatus 38
   julii 39
   nattereri 39
   paleatus 39
Corynopoma riisei 39
Ctenopoma fasciolatum 39
Ctenobrycon spilurus 40

Cynolebias bellottii 40
Danio devario 40
   malabaricus 40
Elassoma evergladei 41
Epalzeorhynchus kallopterus 41
Epiplatys dageti 41
Etroplus maculatus 41
Gasteropelecus levis 42
Gymnocorymbus ternetzi 42
Haplochromis multicolor 42
Hasemania marginata 42
Helostoma temmincki 43
Hemichromis bimaculatus 43
Hemigrammus caudovittatus 43
   armstrongi 43
   erythrozonus 43
   nanus 44
   ocellifer 44
   rhodostomus 44
   unilineatus 44
Heterandria formosa 45
Hyphessobrycon eos 45
   flammeus 45
   heterorhabdus 45
   innesi 46
   metae 46
   ornatus 46
   pulchripinnis 46
   rosaceus 46
   scholzei 46
   serpae 46
Jordanella floridae 47
Kryptopterus bicirris 48
Labeo bicolor 48
Lebistes reticulatus 48
Limia nigrofasciata 48
   melanogaster 49
Macropodus cupanus dayi 49
   opercularis 49
Megalamphodus maglopterus 49
Moenkhausia pittieri 50
Monodactylus argenteus 50
Nannacara anomala 50
Nannaethiops unitaeniatus 50
Nannostomus marginatus 51
   trifasciatus 51
Nematobrycon palmeri 51
Nothobranchius guentheri 51
Pachypanchax playfairii 52
Pterolebias peruensis 52
Poecilia lattipinna 52
   sphenops 53
   velifera 53
Pristella riddlei 53
Pyrrhulina vittata 53
Pseudocorynopoma doriae 54
Pseudotropheus auratus 54

Pterophyllum scalare 54
Rasbora borapetensis 55
   elegans 55
   heteromorpha 55
   maculata 56
   pauciperforata 56
   trilineata 56
Rivulus cylindraceus 56
Scatophagus argus 57
Symphysoden discus 57
Tanichthys albonubes 57
Thayeria obliqua 57
Toxotes jaculator 58
Trichogaster leeri 58
   trichopterus 58
Trichopsis vittatus 58
Xenomystus nigri 59
Xiphophorus hellerii 59
Xiphophorus maculatus 59
   variatus 59

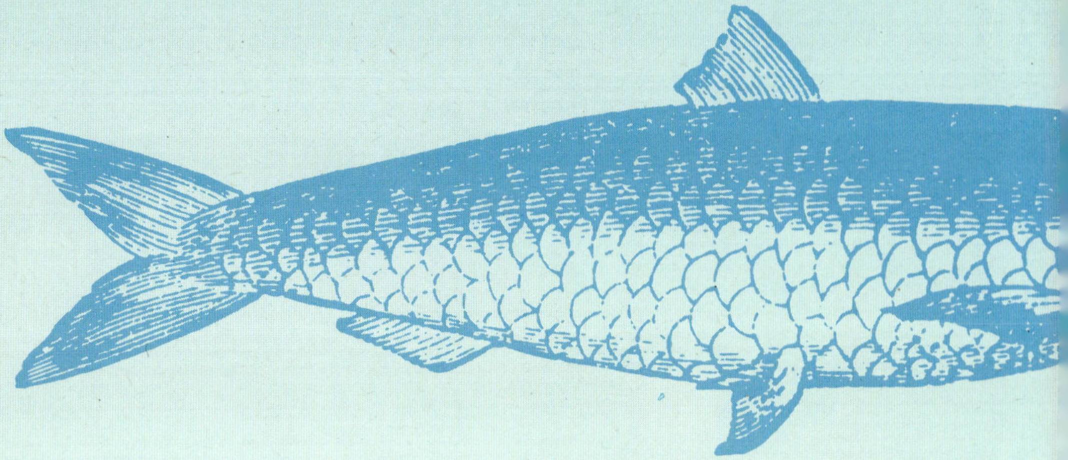

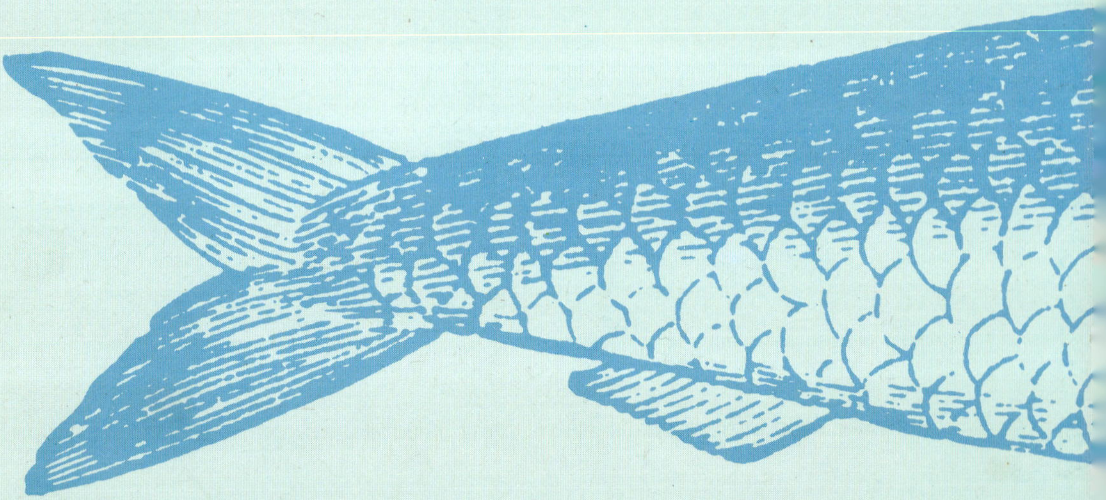